S^{THE}piritual Life

Finding Freedom from Homelessness, Hunger, and Heroin

TYLER G. WALTON

 FriesenPress

One Printers Way
Altona, MB R0G 0B0
Canada

www.friesenpress.com

Copyright © 2021 by Tyler G. Walton
First Edition — 2021

All rights reserved.

Although the author and publisher have made every effort to ensure that the information in this book was correct at press time, the author and publisher do not assume and hereby disclaim any liability to any party for any loss, damage, or disruption caused by errors or omissions, whether such errors or omissions result from negligence, accident, or any other cause.

Adherence to all applicable laws and regulations, including international, federal, state, and local governing professional licensing, business practices, advertising, and all other aspects of doing business in the US, Canada, or any other jurisdiction is the sole responsibility of the reader and consumer.

Neither the author nor the publisher assumes any responsibility or liability whatsoever on behalf of the consumer or reader of this material. Any per¬ceived slight of any individual or organization is purely unintentional.

The resources in this book are provided for informational purposes only and should not be used to replace the specialized training and professional judgment of a healthcare or mental-healthcare professional.

Neither the author nor the publisher can be held responsible for the use of the information provided within this book. Please always consult a trained professional before making any decision regarding treatment of yourself or others.

For more information, email tyler@tylergwalton.com

No part of this publication may be reproduced in any form, or by any means, electronic or mechanical, including photocopying, recording, or any information browsing, storage, or retrieval system, without permission in writing from FriesenPress.

ISBN
978-1-03-910586-7 (Hardcover)
978-1-03-910585-0 (Paperback)
978-1-03-910587-4 (eBook)

1. SELF-HELP, SUBSTANCE ABUSE & ADDICTIONS

Distributed to the trade by The Ingram Book Company

Dedication

To Leif, my little buddy and miracle. You are such an inspiration to me with your love, trust, and intense joy for life. I pray that we can develop and nurture your spirit to be everything God intended for you to be. Love you, little buddy.

To Lois (aka, Louis). You have stuck by me for almost forty years, through thick and thin, in sickness and in health.... I love you deeper and fuller now more than ever. Thank you for your gentle and tender spirit.

Table of Contents

Introduction

Much of what will be written in this book will go against conventional thought, or what has become conventional thought. Some of the content will be deemed controversial. Of course, there will be those who will be offended by my words—the words causing them to stumble. To them I would simply say, "Step higher." What you are about to read may not be conventional today, but it was back in my younger days.

You may be asking, "What are some of these issues?" Many are character traits I have noticed that seem to be lacking. Let's start with character itself. In my estimation, pop culture seems to be more interested in *being* a character than *having* character. The twin evils of pride and arrogance have supplanted humility as the go-to traits people seem to employ.

What we have forgotten is that God gave us one mouth and two ears for a reason. We should use them accordingly, but we don't. People want to hear themselves talk, whether out loud or in print on social media—not that they can hear what they print, but you get the idea. We will discuss the lost art of listening later in the book.

Although I am a Christian, and much (if not all) of my world view is based on a Judeo-Christian mindset, this book will be designed to be read by the general populace, Christian or not. I will make no apologies for any references to the Bible. Please note, I will not be trying to proselytize anyone or convince anyone to adopt my "religious" beliefs.

I should also note that my use of pronouns will be generic, and by that I mean I will be using the term "he" or "him" throughout when I am referring to people in general. I don't have the time nor the energy to try and figure out how to incorporate neutral pronouns into this work.

Chapter 1
MY STORY

So, who am I and what gives me the right to talk about spiritual life? Good questions. Let me begin by saying that today I am not the same man I was ten, twenty, thirty, or forty years ago. Having said that, everything that I went through in those early years were formative, providing a strong—or reasonably strong—foundation for my life today.

My life began like most lives do. I was born to a happy couple in the late fifties. Without going into great detail, and for the sake of time, my first five years were fairly uneventful. At age five, we began to form a pattern that would follow me throughout my school years. We moved from Vancouver, British Columbia, to Calgary, Alberta. The pattern followed my dad's work locations. I attended a total of eleven schools, in four different cities, in two different provinces (or states, for my American friends). We ended up in Kamloops, British Columbia, and stayed there for a total of sixteen years, until I was twenty-seven.

During one of our stays in Calgary, I had the misfortune of being sexually abused by a cousin who was attending technical school in that city. He was smooth. I was only ten, and he was my heroic older cousin: a recipe for disaster. This went on until my dear old dad happened to catch him in an unrelated lie, and after the dust settled, gave him the boot. I never told my parents. This was mainly because the cousin was so smooth that I didn't realize what I was doing was wrong. By the time I was old enough to realize it, I had totally forgotten about it. It wasn't until I was working at a college in Alberta that I realized what had happened. I was in a meeting, and one of the deans confessed to having been sexually abused. I remember thinking to myself, *Wow, am I ever glad that never happened to me!* Then it hit me like a ton of bricks. I immediately went home and told my wife. We prayed together, and I began a history of inner healing, going to many counselors and inner-healing seminars.

Fast forward a few years from the abuse, and we made our final move to Kamloops, B.C., when I was fourteen. I had always been active in sports, and this move was no different. I was involved in most high-school sports, as well as community hockey and baseball. I couldn't get enough of sports. I found that school, schoolwork, and formal education in general got in the way of sports. My grades sucked, except for physical education and related courses.

As I entered my junior year, football took precedence, and some of the other sports fell by the wayside. I loved football and was fairly good at it. Our high-school coach was larger than life, an exceptional strategist and tactician, and very charismatic. He brought out the best and worst in his athletes. Arrogance became the default position of many of us.

After high school, from which I did *not* graduate, I headed south to Texas to play college football. I ended up at Baylor University, where I met some amazing people, many of whom I am still in contact with through social media. Once again, my bad habits with respect to school and education jumped up and bit me in the butt. By my third year, I was invited to leave the school due to my complete lack of grades. Apparently—and I have heard this from reliable sources—you are expected to attend class and maintain a passing grade-point average. My bad.

Upon returning home to Kamloops, I got an above minimum-wage (slightly) job, shipping and receiving for an industrial-supply company. I did fairly well at that job, moved up to counter sales, and ultimately, to outside sales, where I made a fairly decent income. I did this for two years, until I met my future wife.

She was (is) a very attractive woman and very spiritual. She was going to Eastern Europe in the summer of 1982. I was so infatuated that I went along. This was interesting, because she was going there with a mission organization and was going to be on a music team. I have been told, by a missionary no less, that I have a unique voice, or more specifically, that my voice sounds like a horse farting, so the music team was not a good fit for me. Fortunately for me, they also had a "courier" team, one that smuggled Bibles, Christian literature, medical supplies, clothing, and cash to Christians behind the Iron Curtain. With my arm totally twisted, I got coerced into signing up. I quit my job, got engaged, and headed out to Europe for the summer. Such is the power of love.

We returned, got married, spawned a couple of kids, and lived happily ever after. But not. We moved twice, once to Alberta and once back to the lower mainland of British Columbia, to Langley, a suburb of Vancouver. There were housing upgrades along the way, but I felt it important that the kids have a limited number of schools to attend. Both our moves were done before either of them started school. We moved a few times once we settled in Langley, but the kid's education was not affected. The hard part of life was that my poor wife suffered from a serious chemical imbalance that manifested itself in a brutal depression. The poor girl suffered relentlessly for a number of years, until finally, one of the meds she was on actually worked in combination with a host of natural supplements.

Our kids were great. Our firstborn, a boy, struggled in school. He was fairly active, and we were told to medicate him. We did. We hated it, and he hated it. It totally changed his demeanor. The teachers loved it, because he became like the rest of the cookie-cutter kids. It was very unfortunate. This was the early nineties, and we didn't know any better. The sad thing is that the behavioral issues stuck, and he too was invited to leave school. It was so sad, because he was a really bright kid. Ultimately, he ended up in trade school to be a millwright, such being the gift he enjoyed.

Our daughter was a different story, a model student, athlete, musician, and member of student government. She won virtually every award the school had to offer, both as a junior-high student and as a senior-high student. She received athletic scholarships for volleyball and went on to coach in college, and after leaving there, to teach in the public-school system.

Both kids are married with kids of their own, and one on the way, which means I have three and a half amazing grandsons. If I had known grandkids were so much fun, I would have had them first. Such is life.

Between marriage and kids came seminary. Having not graduated from high school, I went to college. Having not graduated from college, where I crammed one year of education into three, I went to grad school. I finally graduated from graduate school/seminary in 1994, cramming a two-year program into two and a half years, which is an improvement over university, at least, earning a Master of Theological Studies in both History and Biblical Studies. I mention this to emphasize my next point, which will shock you regarding the depths to which one individual can fall.

Fast forward from my kids' school years to 2006. I was working as an immigration officer at Vancouver International Airport. During my career there, I had been an intelligence officer as well as an immigration officer. Things were going well there; I was fairly good at my job. I certainly enjoyed the work, though as with most big corporations, morale wasn't the best. Anyway, one day in April, I found myself clearing a Korean Airlines flight from Seoul. It was a Friday afternoon and was to be the last major international flight of the day. It was an uneventful flight to clear, as my main purpose was to ensure all passengers had a valid and subsisting passport. Korean tourists were fairly low risk in that regard. The problem was with Incheon Airport. It was a security nightmare, and many undocumented people showed up transiting through there. The flight cleared, and the flight attendants were egressing the aircraft. As was my custom, I asked them if there was anyone left onboard. Anticipating a negative response, I began walking out with them as I asked this. Unfortunately, they said there was one guy left—of course there was. It was Friday afternoon on a beautiful spring day, and I was getting ready to leave. What could possibly go wrong?

As it turned out, he was a Sudanese National traveling on a Dutch passport. The passport was good. The picture even looked like the passenger, mostly. He was the last to come off the plane and had a slightly suspect photo. The photo was underexposed, so his features didn't stand out, but he did look similar to the photo. He spoke English but not Dutch. That was an issue, as all citizens of the Netherlands were required to speak some Dutch. But he was a refugee, so maybe they'd waived that requirement—or so I thought, or at least hoped. I just wanted to go home. As we began to head downstairs to the customs hall, I asked some innocuous questions to get a feel for the guy. I had his passport in my hand as we walked and talked.

Two things happened as we walked. The first was that he reached over and snatched his passport out of my hand and put it in his breast pocket. *Whoa.* This was shocking. I glared at him, and with rapier-like speed, snatched it back. He asked if I treated everyone like this or just black people. One thing

I'd learned in my tenure with immigration was to never take things personally. It was much easier on the stress levels that way. Suggesting I was a racist, however, crossed a serious line, not to mention raising yet another red flag with this guy. To employ a baseball analogy, he had just struck out, no base on balls; he wasn't getting to first base today, although he might still get into the country. A more in-depth examination would occur once we got down to the immigration office, so there was still hope for him.

The exam raised more questions than it answered. I decided to recommend him removed and a removal order was issued. I then decided to ask him for the truth regarding his passport. He finally admitted that the picture wasn't of him, and that he'd bought the passport. Later, I found out that the passport was provided by a radical and extreme religious group who wanted to do damage to the Winter Olympics, which were to be held in Vancouver. Later viewing of his computer confirmed my suspicions.

As there were no flights back to Seoul that day, we had to wait until Monday. On Monday, when it was time to take him up to his flight, I entered his cell and told him I was going to put handcuffs on him, for his safety, my safety, and the safety of the general public. They would be removed once he was on the plane. That didn't go over too well. A fight ensued. I am not sure what he was thinking, but I subdued him and applied the cuffs.

As I was walking him out, he decided to face plant by "fainting." The next split second was to prove fateful. He was my size (six-foot-one and about 210 pounds) and I decided, without thinking, to catch him and prevent him from bloodying himself and staying his removal. As he was about to hit, I stopped his momentum. Unfortunately for me, I felt (and heard) something go wrong in my lower back. Pain shot through it and down my leg. I lost control of my one leg, and the momentum from catching him sent me face first into the wall across the hall. That triggered some intense pain in my neck. Since my adrenalin was pumping and providing me with a natural painkiller, I soldiered on and finished my task and my day. The next day, I couldn't move. This began a two-year fight with worker's compensation. Just before my fiftieth birthday, I took a pension buyout and "retired" from active service. And so began a dark period in my life, and in the lives of my family.

Later that year, I was in a serious car accident. The doctor I was seeing immediately put me on painkillers, specifically, OxyContin. Fairly significant doses. In fact, he prescribed Oxycodone Instant Release for immediate relief while the OxyContin was kicking in. To make a long story a little shorter, after taking the meds as prescribed, I found myself being cut off the drugs, so I began to crush everything and snort it. Nice. It was then that things went from bad to worse. Since I couldn't get my opiate fix legally, I had to get it from sources not listed in the phone book. In fact, I enlisted a service that I could call who would deliver right to my door in about twenty minutes. The "meds" that I was getting weren't necessarily covered by Pharmacare either. Snorting inevitably led to injecting. I was a full-blown drug addict.

By then, my wife had left, and I had lost everything, including my house, pension, vehicle, savings, family, friends, and was officially a homeless drug addict. Living the dream, or nightmare. Every year, I hit a new low. The question has been asked, "Do you need to hit bottom in order to get out of addiction?" Suffice to say, I not only hit bottom but actually bounced along the bottom, and eventually, dug in even deeper into a veritable pit of despair.

So, the question is this: How does an upstanding, seminary graduate, ex-law enforcement officer/ex-intelligence officer, ex-college coach, ex-pastor, ex-missionary fall to such depths? Before I answer, let me say that the point of the question is to illustrate that it can happen to anyone. No one is exempt. So how does it happen? The simple answer: One day at a time. Longer answer: One bad decision, followed by another and another, and all spawned by an unfortunate event that led to an intense injury. It should be noted that the pain was so intense, my neck spasms so dire, that my blood pressure would spike to stroke levels. How high? As high as 251/212, or so I was told by the triage nurse in the ER. The good part of that was that I was told by my new doctor to go to emergency when that happened. What was good about that is that, when the triage nurse took my blood pressure (three times), she would say "follow me" and lead me past the three to four-hour line up in the emergency room and get me into a bed immediately. Clearly, they didn't want me to die while I was attending their hospital. Too much paperwork. I was then hooked up to an IV with healthy quantities of hydromorphone flowing through my veins. *Mmmmmm … Hydromorphone…. Mmmmmm….* As a good addict, it didn't take me long to abuse the system, including "speeding" up the two-minute drip to make it a two-second drip. This went on for a year before they cut me off. Back to the street drugs.

This lifestyle—if you can call it a life—lasted for 6.75 years. I went from living with my family in a nice five-bedroom home that bordered a park to living in a condo, looking after my mother, who was diagnosed with early onset dementia. I was there for three years until she became more than I could handle. Alzheimer's is a devastating disease, affecting more than just the person concerned. After we moved her into a full-care facility, we sold the condo. Of course, I didn't see any of that money. Devastating for an addict. Anyway, I moved in with my son and his girlfriend. That was a match made in heaven, if heaven resembled hell. My point here, if I may understate things, was that this was a less-than-ideal situation. Three totally dysfunctional adults living together. We bounced around the area for a year and a half until we began squatting in an old trailer. We made a deal with the guy whose land it was that we would clear the land of all the blackberry bushes and make it somewhat respectable. He agreed. I would work in the mornings and do drugs in the afternoon. Sometimes we wouldn't work in the morning but do drugs in both the morning and afternoon.

As the story went, the girl found herself pregnant in the summer of 2016, and by the beginning of December, being the responsible one, she had moved in with her estranged father. To protect the unborn child, she began to come off her drugs by being prescribed Methadone. My son moved in with them at the end of December. Of course, I continued to use, though I was now living on my own, on the streets, in one of the colder winters in recent memory. No more comfy trailer. No more warmth on a cold winter's night. The streets. Living behind a hedge behind the local Staples. Of course, that was short lived, as I was asked to vacate by a very kind maintenance guy. He was supposed to pack up all my junk and toss it in the local dumpster, but instead, he told me about it and recommend I move it if I wanted to keep it. There are always bright spots in the depths of despair. He was one.

So, for the next three months, I was relegated to hitting all-night restaurants for warmth at night; January to March in the Canadian winter necessitated this, and of course, dumpster diving for food. It is important to note that I hadn't lost all my dignity when it came to food. I would only hit dumpsters at one of the local Starbucks and get the prepackaged and sealed food they discarded. Classy.

As fate would have it, my first grandson was born on March 27, 2017. After fifty—yes, five-zero—hours in labor, the little guy showed up. The bruises where they had to use forceps to extract him were beginning to dissipate when I finally went to see him on April fifth. When I finally showed up, my son took me aside and told me that, if I wanted to be a part of the kid's life, I had to leave the drugs behind and clean up. The next day, as it was well after hours when I saw them, I called the detox center and booked myself in. Now, it's not that easy. There was a three to four-week waiting list, but my name went on it. I checked in on May 4, 2017, and have never looked back.

Quick story. As is the standard operating procedure in detox, new admissions see a doctor as soon as possible. I told the doc that I wanted to do the methadone taper. He nodded, then asked me if I was familiar with the success rate of the taper. No. He said it was 100 percent. Being that this was my eighth time in seven years, I knew such was not the case. Taking a cue from my skeptical look, he clarified: 100 percent failure. Nevertheless, it's what I wanted, to be off the stuff once and for all. Then he said something that no other doctor had ever said to me. He said that, if I wanted, I could always go on the maintenance program, and he would monitor me as we weaned me off. *Whoa.* He then told me that he would be coming in for the next three days, until Saturday. Being experienced in the taper program, I felt I could handle it, even though it was only six days, reducing my dose five milligrams per day. Well, by Saturday, I was ready for more than the fifteen mils that I was currently on. The doc saw me, boosted my dosage, and gave me his contact info. And so began my journey into sobriety and recovery.

It is interesting to note that I had tried and failed seven times before; my failure rate was 100 percent. As of this writing, it will be six weeks past my three-year anniversary. So, what made this time different? I had hit bottom years before; indeed, I had dug a pit to sink in even deeper, as I've said, bouncing along the "bottom" of life. Quite simply, I had something to live for now. In a word, there was hope—hope for a relationship with my son and grandson, hope for a restoration of health, hope for a restoration of life. With that hope came support from loved ones. This had been sadly lacking as I had lost all meaningful relationships.

Back to the story. The grandson turned out to be a "miracle baby"—to employ the medical term the doctor used—on a couple of different levels: He was a healthy baby and normal in every way, despite his mother's early pregnancy drug use, and the little guy was also instrumental, indeed the catalyst, in saving me from a life, and likely death, of drug abuse. In that respect, I am happy to report that I am both clean and sober and doing very well; thank you very much.

Small Victories

If there is one thing I have learned, and I have learned many things, it is that things don't just go back to the way they were before the addiction started. Relationships are broken, trust is lost, and to think they can be fixed with a wave of a magic wand is naïve thinking, at best. What took years to establish, and only a few hours to lose, relatively speaking, will take years to restore. As much as this sucks, it is a reality—a fact of life.

The first relationship that I wanted to restore was with my wife. At first, she was leery, having seen me go through detox seven times before. What changed is what I will call the fourth miracle. As fate would have it, we would both end up at the kid's place at the same time. As the little guy got older, he and I really started to bond. He would brighten up when I entered the room, he would smile for me, almost on cue, and he would stop fussing, on those rare occasions that he actually fussed. My wife noticed this and began to warm up to me. As much as she doesn't want to admit it, she just wasn't having the same effect on him. He and I were truly buds. As he began to get older, he began to trust me more. As his trust grew, so did my wife's. We started talking more and spending more time together, rebuilding a relationship that I had done my best to destroy. Although we were still not back living together, we were very close, and close to completely reuniting as a family.

Other relationships followed suit. They were still not fully restored but are much, much better than they were. Of course, it is not nearly as fast as I would like it, but I am eternally grateful that people are willing to forgive and give me yet another chance.

As for my journey through ORT (Opiate Reduction Therapy), on August 27, 2017, I went off methadone altogether. I quickly switched to suboxone, which wasn't nearly as heinous. Then finally, on January 13, 2018, I completely went off suboxone. To quote Martin Luther King Jr., "Free at last! Free at last!" So, my journey in sobriety, which began on May 4, 2017, saw me become both clean and sober on January 13, 2018. One of the side effects of coming off drugs and leaving that lifestyle behind was a 25 percent increase in body weight. I went from 180 lbs. to 225 lbs., mostly in my gut. I have since got this under control and am down to 210 lbs. This is something that I will need to work on. It's funny; when you are not spending every available dollar on drugs, you tend to have extra for food. Novel concept.

Back in my seminary days, one of my profs suggested that I consider doing a PhD. I liked the idea; however, I got stuck with the whole dissertation concept. I didn't want to do a mindless academic-research-type paper, one that was going to gather dust with all the other dissertations at the library. I wanted to do something relevant, something that could be turned into a book that would have some appeal to the general populace. Needless to say, I didn't continue on with my academic career, though the thought of writing a book had been firmly planted in my mind. This was in 1994.

Fast forward once again to 2014. I found myself in recovery at Pacifica Recovery Center in downtown Vancouver. It was a great time. The staff were amazing, very caring and very supportive. I got so much out of my two months there, including coming out clean and sober. Unfortunately, I had the requisite relapse and fell hard once again. The one thing that I got out of Pacifica was a topic for a book. I was voracious in my journaling, and one day, I came up with a topic for a book. I began writing, longhand, an outline for my book. The title I came up with was *Twenty-Eight Days to Spiritual Recovery*. It certainly followed the "twenty-eight-day recovery" motif.

I found out, from one of my favorite people at Pacifica, that the whole concept of a twenty-eight-day recovery program came after the Vietnam War. Many vets came back to the States addicted to heroin. Although many kicked the habit cold turkey when they returned home to their lives and family, there were still many who needed help with recovery. Remember, this was the early seventies. Well, as the story goes, many went to the V.A. and asked what they could do. A study was conducted, and the vets were told the government could fund a twenty-eight-day recovery program, hence, the ubiquitous twenty-eight-day recovery came into being. I believe the original concept originated in the Midwest in the 1950s.

Anyway, as my story goes, the outline that I came up with sat in my journal for another three years as I went through yet another relapse. When I finally entered my final time of sobriety, I purchased an iPad, got a folio with a keyboard to go along with it, and started writing. This was the middle of October 2017. The writing was painfully slow, not because I couldn't type but because I simply had no motivation. By January 12, 2018, after three and a half months, I had completed a total of twelve pages. That's like a page per week. Not good. But January 13, 2018 was the day I entered the final phase of my journey in sobriety. That was the day that I finally came off everything; no more methadone, no more Suboxone, nothing. No more substances again, ever. I was officially done.

January 13, 2018 was a Saturday. On the following Monday morning, at zero dark hundred (0500), I couldn't sleep, so I went down to the local Starbucks with my iPad. I found a comfy chair and started typing, and typing, and typing. By the end of February, a mere six weeks later, I was ready to submit my manuscript, over 180 pages, to a publisher. That was scary. Would they like it? Would they accept it? I called them back east and talked to a lady. She told me how to submit it, went through the potential timeline, etc., and then hung up. Ten minutes later, before I had a chance to submit anything, she called back and told me not to get my hopes up, as they obviously don't accept all manuscripts submitted. Okay. But she did say they would take a look at it. That was all I could ask and expect.

A week later, she left a message on my phone telling me to give her a call. So, with fear and trepidation, I returned her call the next day. She obviously didn't recognize my name and said she would have to get my file. I was starting to feel very disheartened, with every negative voice and negative tape going off in my mind.

"Trevor," she says finally (my name is Tyler). *Great. Clearly my manuscript had a significant impact.* Then she grunts out a "huh," and I am ready to hang up. I felt like Mr. McFly in *Back to the Future* when Marty was telling him to ask out his future wife/mother. Marty said, "I am not sure I can handle that kind of rejection." Well, I was facing that kind of rejection in real time.

"Congratulations," she said, "we have decided to go ahead with your book.[1]" She then said a bunch of other things, but my mind was bouncing off the moon. Being as this was my first book, I'd decided to self-publish. The publishing company seemed decent. They were a full-service outfit, looking after everything from editing, artwork, cover design, printing, both hard copy

....

1   My first book is titled, *Twenty-eight Days to Spiritual Recovery*

and digital, and most importantly, marketing. The downside, of course, is the cost of everything. Even with that, they are very accommodating, offering a monthly pay program.

There we have it. That is most of my story. There are more parts of the narrative that is me, but I want this to be an introduction and a baseline for where I am coming from in this book. As we go further and deeper into the book, more stories and anecdotes will emerge. I hope they are as entertaining as they are enlightening.

Chapter 2
WHY THE SPIRITUAL LIFE?

Why a book on the reclamation of the gift of your spirit? Well, it seems that the spiritual aspect of our lives is sorely lacking. Our culture seems to be fixated on quick fixes, soundbites, and hiding behind our devices and keyboards. We build walls around our souls, and the only doors through which we allow anyone to enter are double thickness with bio-metric access and a numeric key code. In other words, stay out. It's my life, and if you get to know me, you won't like me.

My hope with this book is to allow us time to refocus on our inner, spiritual development, allowing ourselves to become more compatible with ourselves and the community around us. In my experience, we have become a very addictive society, with substance abuse not even making the top-five addictive issues. Think of instant gratification. There is food, sex, gambling, exercise, lying, image, and the list goes on. We want to be filled and satisfied *now*. Instead of dealing with our issues, we hide behind self-made masks, and mask these issues with food, sex, etc., using these items and actions to fill a void that simply can't be filled. To digress for a moment, one of the main causes of substance abuse is childhood trauma. We use drugs to hide from the pain. That trauma can also cause some mental-health issues.

The book will address some personal and spiritual characteristics that will provide some respite from the constant attack and appeal of the carnal, worldly, "out-there" mindsets and worldviews that are so pervasive and destructive in our society. We are going to discuss such topics as establishing peace in one's heart, forgiveness, love, humility, and many more character-oriented traits. We will also be looking at aspects of life that we can do without, traits and learned behaviors that are detrimental to a healthy lifestyle, and developing healthy relationships.

Generally speaking, we call these bad habits—areas of our lives that have become toxic (to coin a phrase) to ourselves and toxic to those around us. Another word for toxic is poisonous—poisonous to our inner selves, and poisonous to those around us. "Poisonous," of course, is an adjective describing a substance that can cause illness or death if ingested, or even if it comes in contact with the body. Some negative traits and bad habits have that spiritual effect, not only on us as individuals but on those who come in contact with us. And by spiritual, I am referring also to the emotional and psychological.

We will demystify the concept of "tough love," redefine it, and give some guidelines on how to implement tough love. This is mainly in response to dealing with drug addicts in the family, but can also be adapted to any difficult situation. We will look at the spiritual foundations of love and relationships, and offer some spiritual insights to relationship building, healing, and restoration.

Perhaps the biggest area of discussion, one that will permeate this work and one that is foundational in all of life, is humility. Humility is a lost art of inner discipline, of an inner mindset. It is a discipline that can be developed by the most cynical and arrogant of people, one that turns people from being jerks to live with to being joys to live with. Trust me on this one.

In conclusion to this introduction, allow me to state unequivocally that I am a born-again Christian. This will be written from a Christian perspective, and there may be quotes and Bible verses used. Having said that, this is not an attempt at proselytizing, I am not trying to convert anyone or suggest that anyone adopt my Christian belief system. I make no apology for any of this. If it causes you to stumble, my suggestion is that you step higher.

I trust you will enjoy this book.

Chapter 3
IN THE BEGINNING

No, this is not a polemic on the creation of the world. Rather, it is a look at our own human condition. When we look at how our lives began, how they developed and formed, leading us to be the people that we are today, we can see how the need for inner healing is so necessary.

So, let's go back to the beginning. Birth. The whole process is a traumatic experience for everyone. When my wife was at the hospital delivering our second child—we are not going to talk about my involvement in the first—she found it was a whirlwind delivery. At 1415 hrs., her water broke. I raced home from work, picked her up, and raced her to the hospital. From the time of her water breaking to the time our daughter popped out was exactly two hours. Full on labor, pushing, and pain. To ease the pain, she would sit on the toilet. I would go in with her and noticed immediately that her breathing was off. So, I performed my role as the dutiful dad and had her follow my exaggerated breathing. As a dutiful mom, she actually followed my exaggerated breathing example. By the time the example actually registered with her, I was in pass-out mode from hyperventilating. That was so traumatic. For me. My wife? She was kind of preoccupied at the moment and didn't pay me much attention.

I am being totally facetious in this example. My wife was going through a type of hell on earth, my daughter was making her way down the exceptionally narrow birth canal, being squeezed out like a ... well, being seriously squeezed, and I am talking about me and my breathing. Really? I mean, who does that?

What I really want to discuss and point out is the trauma experienced by the child in the birth process. If we think about it, something so natural, so beautiful, can be the most harrowing experience many of us will encounter. We start in a nice, warm, peaceful environment. It's dark. There is a never-ending supply of nutrition. There are pleasant, muted sounds. Then we enter a dark, long, very cramped tunnel. What the heck is this? It's so tight and cramped, long and narrow. We are getting pushed against our will towards some unruly, bright light. It's so bright, and what is that loud, obnoxious noise? There are loud voices, and some woman is periodically screaming.

Interestingly, the screams subside, then pick up again. They seem to pick up when the tunnel gets tighter and the squeezing intensifies. Then as the light is getting brighter, some hands grab our head and start pulling. Not hard, but we can feel it. Then it gets cold as we seem to move out of the warmth of the host body and into the cold, cruel world. Then some guy slaps our bare butt. *Owww!* At least they wrapped us in some warm blankets. That's not so bad.

And so, after a significantly long time, at least in baby hours, that trauma comes to an end. But just when we think it's safe, the real work begins. How does it begin? These early days begin to form the basis for our early years. We learn that if we cry, we get action. If we get hungry, we cry and soon enough, we get some food. If we mess our diaper, we cry and it gets changed. In fact, the louder we cry, the quicker we get stuff, be it food, attention and love, or a "dipe-dipe" change. We also learn that if we smile and "coo," the big people smile and "coo." We learn that we can control the big people by our actions, and we learn that at a very young age.

As we get older, from about two to five years of age, these behavioral issues are intensified, especially if the big people don't clue into our little attention-getting charades. Don't get me wrong, there are times when toddlers seem to be acting up, but sometimes the only way they can communicate that something is wrong is by crying. The older toddlers may cop some serious attitude when something is physically wrong, and it is up to the big people in their lives to discern behavioral issues versus medical issues.

As an aside, just the other day, I came home after a very physically demanding day. My lower back and neck were spasming, and I had the mother of all headaches. I had had these years before, and before too long, checked my blood pressure: 170/123. Not great. I fell asleep on the couch, and my wife woke me up around eight fifteen. I awoke with a start and growled at her, then promptly fell back to sleep. She woke me up an hour later. Once again, I awoke with such a start that it scared her, such was the pain and effects of the high blood pressure.

Needless to say, the next morning I checked my blood pressure, and it was 232/146, with the headache still in high gear. Off to emergency. Anyway, when I was all done and things were back to normal, she said to me that now she understood my seemingly insane behavior the night before. My point is this: I had come full circle as a human in that I was acting out physical/medical issues, not unlike when I was a toddler. It was a good reminder for both of us, especially now that we have three grandkids three and under.

As we get older, sometimes the behavioral issues become more subtle. Tantrums give way to pouting. Pouting gives way to acting out. Acting out takes on various forms, including but not limited to silence, ignoring, not cleaning your room, not doing any chores, doing a poor job of chores, and the list goes on. Then there is the public shaming. I remember being in a Walmart looking for some baby stuff. There was a mom with a six-year-old. The kid was seriously acting out, laying on the floor, waiting for Mom's attention. As fate would have it, he was laying right in front of where I was looking. The mom in question was having none of his behavior, ignoring his antics. The kid wasn't giving up, holding fast to his rebelliousness. I looked down at him, and he looked up at me. Our eyes locked for a second, and shaking my head, I simply asked him, "Is this working for you?" I wasn't sure if he would understand, but I said it anyway. Well, he did understand. He got up, sheepishly, and with head hung low, rejoined his mom.

Which brings me to my next point: Kids are far smarter than we give them credit for. They are very quick to figure things out, especially when it comes to getting what they want. As an aside, my three-year-old grandson, Leif—yes, named after the famous Viking explorer who discovered North America five hundred years before Columbus (490-ish years—understands me full well when I talk to him like I talk to adults. Okay, maybe not exactly like I talk to adults, but I talk in full sentences, using simple words, and I talk slowly, emphasizing key words. Just because he can't talk doesn't mean that he doesn't understand.

Back to kids getting their way and the lengths they will go to for it. Actually, now that I think about it, I am not going to discuss that any further. As a (mostly) mature adult, I have come to the conclusion that more bees are caught with honey than with vinegar. What I mean by this is that toddlers, pre-schoolers, primary-school kids, and adolescents, anyone really, respond far better to positive re-enforcement than to negative, power-infused demands. Recently, I did a very unscientific study with Leif. We wanted to get him to eat something that he wasn't really into. After he took a taste, I began to clap and cheer and encourage him. Guess what? When I presented him with the next spoonful, he happily and willingly took the next bite.

I started doing this for everything, and lo and behold, I got him to do stuff that his parents couldn't get him to do. Of course, it worked so well that I quit doing it, and the results were telling. He stopped being the cooperative little buddy that I knew and loved and started exhibiting a stubborn streak. Back to being the cheerleader, back to the positive re-enforcement, back to the happy, cooperative little buddy that we all know and love. One more thing about dealing with kids: I find it is far more spiritually productive when we *empower* kids rather than try to *control* them. Let them have a stake in the process. Teach them to think and make decisions for themselves, rather than physically and verbally doing everything for them.

Perhaps overcoming the negative human condition that we all develop is as simple as being treated with patience, love, and respect. Perhaps it's just a matter of adults behaving like adults. As an immigration officer, I was yelled at, insulted, threatened, and generally talked to in a derogatory manner, not to mention being lied to on a daily basis. I remember being asked by some of the younger staff how I maintained my composure. After a moment's thought, I simply said that I didn't take it personally. These people had no equity in my life; they meant nothing to me or my personal well-being. They didn't know me and had no right nor authority to contribute anything to my life. Furthermore, I didn't know their story, what was causing the outburst, or why they were acting out.

I know that is a little different with our kids. They do have some equity; they do mean something to us, and they can affect our personal wellbeing. But it is the mature adult in us that has to rise above the "I hate you, Dad," and overcome the desire to lash out in anger and get our licks in. "No kid of mine is going to talk to me like that." That may be the underlying thought, but that needs to be manifested in love, patience, and maturity.

This leads to another aspect of the *human condition* that I need to address: the role of the parent in forming the child's behavior. As was mentioned earlier, I have found it is far more productive, and conducive to raising a healthy child, to empower the child rather than control the child. Overbearing and controlling parents will produce overbearing and controlling children. This is especially true with the firstborn. The way the firstborn is treated will be the way they treat their younger siblings most of the time. This can have some disastrous effects in the family dynamic. If, on the other hand, they are treated with respect and dignity, being gently taught and handled, they will usually respond in kind.

If there is one piece of advice that I can give to anyone it is this: The precedents that you set with your children, whether good, bad, or indifferent, will have lasting ramifications. Choose wisely. Not every decision needs to happen in a split second. Take your time. In most cases, time is your friend.

Another thing to remember is that kids are resilient. They can bounce back from pretty much anything. They are loving and forgiving. Having said that, don't violate their trust, if at all possible. If you do, you need to have a serious heart to heart. If you want any success in raising your child, that trust has to be restored; the child has to think it is safe to be around you, talk to you, and open up to you in any way. Trust me; this is critical as the kids enter the teen years.

Chapter 4
HAVING CHARACTER. . .

Rather than *being* a character

I am sure this isn't anything new, and I am sure I will mention it again later. Unfortunately, we are living in an age where the opposite is true. I have said it in the past, will say it now, and will likely say it in the future: We are living in a soundbite society, where we seem to want to hear ourselves talk, usually not out loud but rather hiding behind a monitor and keyboard. We seem to find solace in being critical of people we have never met simply because we can. We give no regard to the feelings of others with the words we print. It would seem as though we are only interested in the number of "likes" we get or how many times we get "retweeted."

Having character seems to have lost its appeal as a virtue to be aspired to. One of the reasons for this, I have concluded, is because of the dubious role models we hold in high esteem. Instead of being content with who we are, we seem to want to live vicariously through others. Unfortunately, these "others" likely don't want the job of being emulated; they are quite content living out their own dysfunction. But emulate them we do, usually to our own overall detriment. It may feel good at the time, but the void that is within each of us remains a void. Indeed, we seem to avoid filling this void, looking (as the song goes) in all the wrong places, and to all the wrong people.

So, what will it take to change this? When I was going to school in Texas, I worked in a pool hall. The old guy I worked for was your typical, wise, old, and experienced man. He told me a story one day about an old farmer who was sitting on his porch with his dog. The dog was yowling away. When the farmer's buddy came by, he asked why the dog wouldn't stop yowling. The farmer thought about it a while and replied, "'Cause it's laying on a nail." "Why doesn't he move?" the friend asked. The farmer pondered the question and replied, "I guess it isn't bugging him enough."

Such is life. We don't change, even though we know we need to, because what we need to change isn't bothering us enough. I have been asked a number of times if, when I was using drugs, I had to hit bottom to get better. I have given this considerable thought and have come to the conclusion that, no, hitting bottom had precious little to do with getting out of the trap of addiction. By this, I mean, there is no "bottom," per se. For me, I thought my bottom came when I started abusing drugs. It only went downhill from there. Seriously, though, going from respectable, contributing member of society to homeless, dumpster-diving drug addict was a fairly precipitous fall. And it's not like you actually hit bottom, dust yourself off, and get over it. No, you hit bottom, bounce, hit bottom, bounce, hit bottom, etc. Of course, each subsequent bounce isn't as high as the previous bounce. With me, there weren't many bounces; in fact, I not only rested on the bottom for a significant amount of time but I began to dig a pit to go even deeper and lower. It's one of the downsides of being an overachiever. I wasn't satisfied with how far I had fallen. There were always new lows to conquer. Please realize, gentle reader, that, although I am being facetious, this is not altogether inaccurate.

So, what happened to cause me to sink to such depths? After all, I thought I had an above-average level and depth of character. I had a loving family, a respectable job, and I was known and respected in the community. What happened? I would like to say it was all because of the pain, which led to painkillers, which led to abuse, which led to self-medicating with non-prescription "meds." I would like to say that, but I can't in all honesty. No, apparently—and by "apparently" I mean really—there were some unresolved character issues that needed to be dealt with.

There is a story from antiquity that I didn't understand until I went through my addiction. The story is about the Babylonian king, Nebuchadnezzar. At the height of his rule and splendor, he had a divine visitation, and to make a long story short, went through seven years of homeless mindlessness. He didn't take care of himself, and his hygiene tanked. He was no better than a beast, or cattle. It wasn't until he learned whatever he was supposed to learn that he was restored to both physical and mental health. Oddly enough, my demise into drugs lasted almost seven years (6.75, to be precise). I had virtually lost my mind, did things I would have never expected of myself, lived like a junkyard dog (my apologies to junkyard dogs), and gave little or no thought to others or to my hygiene. It wasn't until I, like Nebuchadnezzar before me, lifted my eyes to heaven that my life was restored. Consider this to be my outworking of steps two and three from Alcoholics Anonymous.

Anyway, when I finally came out of my drug-induced stupor, there were some character flaws that were revealed to me that I needed to work on. Not the least of these was a critical and judgmental spirit that had been solidly ingrained in my psyche. This came from a place of arrogance and superiority. I remember a time when I was just married, in my mid-twenties. I was with a mentor, and I said to him, "I have to confess, I really struggle with pride."

He laughed out loud and said to me, "Really? What do you have to be proud about?"

Hmmmm. What, indeed. When I finally realized this enough to deal with it, I was brought low, emotionally and psychologically. Realizing that you have lived your life as a complete idiot tends to have that effect on you.

Following this revelation came the next character flaw I needed to deal with. It was the feeling of entitlement that I had developed years before the drugs began. I'm pretty sure this came from the pride and arrogance that I had developed. This sense of entitlement, when I was confronted with it, was possibly the most offensive thing I have ever heard. The reason being that I held those who thought they were entitled in such low regard, and to be listed as one of them was mind-numbing—not that I felt I was entitled to the same stuff as they were, just that I was entitled to anything.

I would like to say that becoming aware of these character deficiencies solved all my problems; it didn't. Fact is, it seemed to make matters worse, psychologically and emotionally. But this was a good thing. I look at this as a surgery for the soul. It is said that awareness is the beginning of the healing process. In my experience, this is true. One of the main aspects of character development is the willingness to allow our character to be developed. As I continue my discussion on the spiritual life, I will delve further into the inner workings of character development.

Chapter 5
BEING MINDFUL OF MINDFULNESS

All good self-help books should employ at least one aspect of pop culture, employing at least one buzz word that everyone can relate to. I may as well get mine out of the way from the outset. "Mindfulness" and being mindful are likely to be going out of vogue by the time this book hits the presses. Oh well.

Let me begin by quoting a paper that was given to me when I entered the Pacifica Recovery Center in 2014. The author was listed as "Anonymous." It went like this:

> I will be mindful of my thoughts, because my thoughts will lead to my words;
>
> I will be mindful of my words, because my words will lead to my actions;
>
> I will be mindful of my actions, because my actions will lead to my habits;
>
> I will be mindful of my habits, because my habits will lead to my character;
>
> I will be mindful of my character, because my character will lead to my destiny.

When I entered recovery, I was at one of my absolute low points in life. The first person I met had a profound impact on me. She exuded both confidence and humility. She had an empathy that touched my soul at a deep level. She is the one who gave me this quote. And so began my journey into recovery.

The year was 2014—Aug 1, 2014, to be precise. I had just entered the recovery center from the detox center and had been off methadone for three days. To say that I was feeling *it* would be an understatement. I was dying. I couldn't sleep, my joints were aching, and my flesh was crawling. Brutal. I went down and talked with the lady whom I'd first met when I arrived to see if I could see the doctor when he came in on Friday. It was now Thursday. We had a great chat and seemed to make a spiritual connection. She led our morning sessions, and I hung on her every word, her every action. I learned so much from her—not so much from what she said but from how she behaved, how she handled herself, and how she handled us.

I always went back to that first meeting when she gave me the "mindfulness" paper. Obviously, it had a profound effect on me. From actually practicing mindfulness came the outline for my first book, pages upon pages of journaling, and copious notes from our sessions. Further to this, I have found that practicing mindfulness, or awareness, does not come naturally for me. It is a discipline that I have to practice. I find I have to be mindful to get into a state of constant mindfulness. Novel concept. What I am saying, seriously, is that it takes discipline to live in a state of mindfulness. Please note, I will be using the term "awareness" interchangeably with mindfulness.

Thoughts

I find it very easy to allow my thoughts to get away from me. I'm sure you have heard it said, "He's his own worst enemy." Next to the definition of this phrase is my picture, not to put too fine a point on it. On top of my mind, wandering aimlessly through the wilderness, I have an inscrutable propensity to overthink things. By things, I mean everything, from the serious and substantial to the inconsequential and inane.

King Solomon, in the Book of Proverbs, says, "For as he thinks in his heart, so is he." (Proverbs 23:7, New King James Version). Heady stuff from the wisest man to ever live. As we think, so we become. Our thoughts shape us and mold us into the men and women we see in the mirror every day. If we pause long enough, how many of us see a reflection that is worthy of the ideals we had as kids? Often, we tell ourselves lies that we know are lies, but we tell ourselves them nevertheless. In fact, we tell ourselves these lies often enough that we actually begin to believe them. At least we begin to justify our poor behavior as a result. This is how our thoughts become our words.

If we can master the discipline of controlling our thoughts, we can then experience the first vestiges of hope in controlling our tongues. Let me explain what I mean by "controlling our thoughts." Random thoughts, negative thoughts, and positive thoughts will bombard our consciousness every minute of every day. For the record, there is no hope in absolute control over this. What we can control, however, is what we do with the thoughts once they enter our consciousness.

Think of our consciousness as a war. The combatants in this war are our thoughts. The battlefield is our minds. Positive thoughts and truth are our allies. Negative thoughts and lies are our enemies. As life goes on and the battle rages in our minds, we (as warriors of life) need to take captive every negative thought and bring it into submission. The best way to do this is to slow ourselves down a little. We live in such a fast-paced society that, when a negative thought hits us, we simply ignore it, putting it off until later. That's not dealing with it, nor is it bringing anything into submission. If we think about it, our busyness, or sense of busyness, is another enemy we need to face head on. More on that later.

The enemy begins to gain a foothold when we give these thoughts over to words.

Words

To continue the battlefield metaphor, words can be both our friends and our enemies. In fact, the tongue has been likened to a rudder on a ship, in terms of how something so small can control something so big. It has also been likened to a fire, one that can heat and warm, and cook food, but can also destroy an entire forest, our houses, and all our possessions. Yet again, and a little more serious, it has been said that the tongue is like a fountain. How can pure water and bitter water come out of the same fountain?

Hopefully, we can see the power of the tongue and the words that flow from it. When our negative thoughts give way to negative words, we begin a slide down a slippery slope that will lead to destruction. These words don't even have to be audible. When they form in our minds—the battlefield—then we either duck for cover, take the hit, or fire back. I will liken the ducking for cover to ignoring the negative words. Taking the hit of the negative words simply means that we believe the words and allow them to take root in our souls and minds and allow them to fester and infect our inner being.

If we need to take our thoughts captive, we certainly need to take our negative words captive. Although we can keep our negative thoughts and words to ourselves, before long our words will get the best of us, and we will begin spewing toxic vitriol. It may sound cool at first, but let me assure you, those sounds are fleeting. Once again, it is going to take an incredible amount of discipline to control our words. One of the most rewarding things I have encountered since embarking on this spiritual journey is the feeling I have experienced doing battle with myself. There have been victories and defeats, or to paraphrase Jim McKay on *Wide World of Sports* from the seventies, I have experienced the joy of victory and the agony of defeat.

The thing to remember here is that our thoughts and inaudible words are our own. We don't share them with anyone but ourselves, and ultimately, with God. We can hide behind these thoughts and words and live in our own little fantasy world. Once our words leave our minds, well … let's just say you can't unring that bell. The toothpaste is out of the tube and ain't goin' back in. The bottom line is that, if the words are destructive, they will leave a mark on whomever they were intended for. In this case, our aim is impeccable. We hit our targets, and the depths of the wounds we create are only dependent on the person receiving them. If they are mature, disciplined, and even spiritual, the damage may be mitigated somewhat. On the other hand, if they are not any of these, the next place you see them is in the triage ward of the local hospital, figuratively speaking. Such is the importance of self-discipline and self-control.

Actions

This is where things get real. If negative spoken words are bad, actions only multiply the damage. I remember years ago waiting in a doctor's office for an appointment. There was a poster on the wall that caught my attention. It said, simply, "The smallest good deed is better than the grandest of intentions." I'm sure we have heard it said that "actions speak louder than words."

No one will dispute this or even argue about it. We can say things in passing, but it takes an effort, time out of our day, to actually do something.

The more we speak something out, the more we believe it. Spiritually speaking, when we start to give voice to the lies, acting out the lies is only a matter of time. Society is morphing downwards from a soundbite society, where we want to hear the sound of our own voices, or see our words immortalized in print on social media, to a society where we are going to put action behind our words. The world is becoming a protest zone. Left protests right, and right protests left. When the two meet, there is often bloodshed and police intervention.

Just as our words give way to our actions, so our actions give way to habits—habits, of course, being the constant and consistent performance of a behavior or action. We can experience both good and bad habits. Bad habits are usually the ones we know we should quit but don't. By becoming mindful of our thoughts and words, we can be more in control of our actions. Being aware of what we are thinking and saying greatly minimizes any negative actions and behaviors that become detrimental to healthy relationships, both with others and with ourselves.

It is essential to a healthy spiritual life to be at peace with yourself. It is foundational to be at peace in your spirit to also be at peace with others. It is our behavior towards others, the way we treat them, the things that we do, or our actions, that will determine how they respond or react to us.

It is important to note the difference between a response and a reaction. A response in medical terms usually means that the patient is doing well with the medication or treatment that has been administered. If the patient is not doing well, they are having a reaction. So, response = positive; reaction = negative.

Like thoughts and words, our actions can be either a blessing or a curse to others or to ourselves. So often, we act without thinking, by the seat of our pants, much to the chagrin of the people we know and love. A spiritual person is not in a rush to act; rather, the spiritual person wants to do what is right, not only for him but for all around. Before we do something, what if we stopped for a moment and thought of the ramifications of our action. Now, I understand that there are times when immediate action is required, even demanded. These situations are exceptional in nature and shouldn't be confused with a "seat of the pants" lifestyle.

Habits

As was mentioned earlier, when the same action is repeated time and time again, a habit is formed. There have been volumes written about the need for good habits and how to form good habits. There has been much written about how to break bad habits.

One of the main, fundamental ways to determine your habits is through awareness of who you are, your thoughts, your words, and your actions. I can't stress enough the need to slow our lives down, allot some alone time each and every day to recharge and renew our spirits. During this "me" time, we can review the previous days thoughts, words, and actions. We can then make the proper adjustments, so these aspects of our lives are enhanced, if positive, or eliminated, if negative.

Meditation is not just for the yogis and gurus of Eastern Mysticism. Getting into the habit of meditation, usually before the day begins and after the day ends, is a habit worthy of a healthy spiritual life. Meditation on the upcoming day—conditioning our minds for what we may experience during the day and how we will handle various situations we encounter—is one of the more beneficial aspects of my life in recovery. Further, taking the time to reflect on the day's events at the end of the day, reviewing successes in behavior and thought, as well as the areas that I can improve on (read: failures), is a great way to prepare for a good night's rest and prep for a new day.

When we become aware that our actions may, indeed, be turning into bad habits, there are some steps that can be taken, not the least of which is establishing in our minds an alternate behavior that is acceptable to us, which can be acted out instead of the bad behavior. It is imperative that we don't beat ourselves up if we slip. We are certainly not perfect and shouldn't treat ourselves as though we are. I mean, seriously, if we slip up, the very presence of the slip-up indicates non-perfection. Let's just accept our imperfections and see if we can't improve and become better tomorrow, or next time. Sometimes, one of the first gifts we can give ourselves is a break.

Don't get me wrong; it's okay to be upset if we make a bonehead move, especially if we make the same move over and over after wanting to break this habit. What's not okay is to allow our distress to become an emotional trap that sucks the life out of us. This emotional trap is usually riddled with shame and toxic guilt (more on toxic guilt later). Trust me, it is better to do without the emotional roller coaster incumbent with shame.

It is time for the introduction of a mantra that seems to work quite well. I learned this in recovery, and it was part of my Cognitive Behavior Training (CBT). My counselor simply told me to say, whenever a craving came along, "I am having a craving. It is a thought about using drugs, but it is just a thought. Thoughts have no power or control over me. I simply say 'no' to this craving and will not succumb to its suggestion." Usually, by the time I had finished this mantra, the craving was gone, and I didn't act on it. Miraculous. Such is the power of thoughts, words, and actions over our bad habits. The craving can be for anything: food, sex, gambling, lying, gossip, drugs, or alcohol. There is no limit on what is affected. If it has a negative effect, we can take charge over it and eliminate it from our daily lives.

Make no mistake; breaking habits takes work. This work can be exceptionally difficult at first, with our efforts fraught with failure and disappointment. If it were easy, anyone could do it, and in the hands of a lesser person, gentle reader, I would be concerned. But you can do this.

I gave up a serious heroin and crystal-meth addiction, where I injected the dope intravenously. At my lowest, if I went more than six hours without some dope, I began to experience dope-sickness—or withdrawal, to the uninitiated. When that starts to set in, thinking goes out the window, and you have but one thing on your mind. Trust me, you are not thinking about that one thing but acting on instinct to get that one thing, which becomes the default. The longer you go without, the stronger the impulse to get the drugs is, and the more desperate and brazen are the actions taken to get money to purchase the drugs. Societal norms, the law, and your reputation are all left at the door; you are in unchartered territory. I have been there, usually a few times a week. I did some shameful things of which I am not proud. I will not dignify my actions with any description; suffice to say that I never stole off any individual person. Read into that what you will; you will likely be right. The good news for me, personally, is that I never had to serve any time for my behavior.

I say all of this only to provide you with some hope. The worst of addictions can be overcome and beaten, kicked to the curb, and left behind in the dust. But is a mantra all that it will take? In my experience, the mantra is a great first step. In fact, expect the mantra to evolve; it did for me. You see, I take steps two and three of the twelve steps very seriously: I "came to believe that a power greater than ourselves could restore us to sanity" and I "made a decision to turn our will and our lives over to the care of God as we understood Him." For me, my shelved faith needed restoring. For my son and his girlfriend, they didn't. Their belief system is quite different from mine.

In fact, if you look closely at the twelve steps, the concept of "Higher Power/God" is directly mentioned in six of the steps and a "spiritual awakening" is mentioned in a seventh. Apparently, the founders of the twelve steps recognized the need for having someone or something greater than ourselves, someone or something benevolent when we are being led and guided out of the pit of despair that is addiction.

Back to my mantra. In July of 2017, I was facing some serious craving issues in my life. I had been sober for three months—usually the time in the lives of most addicts when relapse rears its ugly head. Relying on my awareness of what was going on in my body and mind, not to mention what was going on in my environment, I was facing some serious temptations. On a whim, I began to pray to God, inserting him in my mantra. It went like this: "Father, I am weak (step one), and I don't know how long I can withstand these temptations. I know that you can deliver me from this evil substance abuse (step two). You are strong when I am weak. Therefore, I submit these cravings to you, that you would renew my mind and restore me (step three)." Guess what? He answered this prayer. The next time a strong craving came upon me, I prayed the same prayer with the same results. Now this may sound very pithy and trite, but for a recovering addict who is being inundated with powerful cravings, it is very significant.

A month later, I came off Methadone altogether and went on Suboxone. Four and a half months after that, on January 13, 2018, I was free and clear of everything. Both clean and sober. Needless to say, I haven't looked back.

Admittedly, this is an extreme type of bad habit—a bad habit that exercised control and manipulation over my entire person. What I am getting at in this whole story is that there is no habit that can't be broken. If there is any hope, it is that there is no substance available that can totally control your life forever. There is no habit so bad that it can't be overcome. If you are stuck, take heart; with a lot of hard work and determination, you can be free.

Of course, this also goes for any loved ones who are stuck in the insanity of addiction or bad habits. No one has to be stuck forever.

Character

I've said it once, and I'll say it again, "The world needs more people with character than those who are being characters." The problem is—and I am oversimplifying here—that people seek the easy way out. They allow life to happen to them. Character needs to be developed; it takes work. Developing character means that we will be changing from the inside out. Change is never fun or easy, but it is necessary in the development of character.

Time for a quick anecdote: In 2014, I found myself attending the Pacifica Residential Recovery Center in Vancouver, B.C. One of the young girls who had gone through intake with me was complaining about something at home. As I was not part of the conversation, I just listened intently. Then she said, "I am not going to change. If they can't accept me for who I am, to hell with them."

I thought for a second about the ramifications of this statement. A second later, I said, "Sorry to hear that." She then went on to tell me she wasn't going to change, that she was happy the way she was, and that she wasn't into people pleasing, to which I simply asked, "Why are you here, learning to overcome your addiction?" I went on to explain that it was likely to change some part of her life, and help her to become a better person. I then went on a rant. Of course, you don't want to change just to please others. But living in peace with others isn't such a bad thing. It is a give and take proposition. Changes have to be made on both sides. I suggested that the likely reason she was in recovery was that there were serious character flaws in her life, her relationships were in the sewer, and the only people who would give her the time of day were her drug dealer or people who wanted something from her. Not a very appealing lifestyle, and she might want to reconsider her rigid stance on change.

Such is the essence of character. If we are to be true to ourselves, then change is to be a constant staple of our lives. The technical term for not changing is being stuck. So, what does getting "unstuck" look like? For our discussion here, it is a matter of breaking bad habits, making healthy decisions, living in a cooperative community situation, getting along with others, and getting along with yourself. Character means you can get up in the morning, look yourself in the mirror, and have no regrets for your behavior. It means that, before you go to bed at night, you can look yourself in the mirror and feel good about how you behaved during the day. You can sleep in peace.

Destiny

We have heard it said that life isn't a destination but a journey. True enough. There are some differences in the terms "destiny" and "destination" that should be made. The main difference being that the destination is rather final in nature. A destiny, on the other hand, is more fluid.

As we can see from this little study on mindfulness, our destinies can be affected if we are not careful with our thoughts, words, actions, and the like. It is amazing how the smallest event today can have the most profound of effects tomorrow.

Mindfulness and awareness are disciplines in life that we have to take seriously if we are to survive as successful, contributing members of society. Being aware of the issues in our lives and our behavior is no small task. It takes time, patience, and discipline. Rest assured; the effort is worth it.

Points to Ponder

1. *What thoughts do I need to get control of that are negatively affecting my spiritual growth, keeping me enslaved?*

2. *How are my words hurting myself and others? What are some tools I can use to control my negative words?*

3. *What negative actions are present in my life that shouldn't be?*

4. *How are my bad habits keeping me and others down?*

5. *What are the main character traits that are affected by my bad habits? How do I break these habits?*

Chapter 6
HUMILITY

I will leave arrogance and pride behind
and adopt a lifestyle of humility, putting
the interests of others ahead my own

When we discuss our spirituality, one characteristic is foundational. Although there are many worthy characteristics that we will discuss, there is none, in my mind, more important, and neglected, than humility. Humility is when we empty ourselves *of ourselves,* or at least, the self that we have become. Humility becomes the first step in our metamorphosis into our true spiritual selves. This is why I began the process with awareness. Our personal awareness—indeed, our spiritual awareness—will become our default state in life once we adapt to, and adopt, the philosophies of the spiritual life as outlined in this book.

As was mentioned above, humility is when we empty ourselves. For many, it is about going back to a time of abject innocence in our lives. Often, this is remembering when we were at our best as children: innocent, idealistic, unstoppable. Of course, there may be those who didn't have that type of experience as kids. In that case, you are in the enviable position of reconstructing who you would want to be from scratch. Perhaps a better subtitle for this book would have been *Reconstructing Your Spiritual Self.* Either way, each of us will find ourselves in a rebuilding, or renovating, period of our lives.

When I was much younger and far more immature, like two years ago, I used to think I was the most humble guy I knew. It wasn't until my wife asked me, "Did you hear what you just said?" after making some random, arrogant comment, that I took the time to reflect on my abject arrogance. I found it difficult to show true humility when I spent so much time talking about how humble I was. Seriously, most of what I have said in this paragraph is said tongue in cheek. The one thing that is fairly accurate is my arrogant behavior in life in general.

When I began to confront my arrogance, I began to realize that people didn't really appreciate me for who I was. All they saw was a cocky, arrogant man who thought, perhaps, that he was better than everyone else. It started to bother me that they didn't see the good in me. Of course, the fault wasn't with them; it was with me. I was unaware, or didn't want to acknowledge, my shortcomings. To acknowledge them would mean I was less than perfect and *would need to change.*

Before I get too far into this discussion, it is important to provide a working definition of the word "humility." There are many definitions that are negative—ones that explain what humility isn't, what's not present. For example, there is no pride or arrogance in humility. There is definitely no selfishness involved.

A quick word on selfishness as it relates to addiction, any addiction, even behavioral addictions. Succumbing to and living out your addictive behaviors is possibly the most selfish thing people can do. When I was heavy into my addiction, I didn't think of anyone or anything other than myself and my need to satisfy my "needs." This was the epitome of selfish behavior on my part. There were certain payoffs for me when I acted out my addiction: I felt a certain amount of euphoria, as in many cases the drugs alleviated the "dope sickness" that sets in after a prolonged period without dope, and I could experience a brief escape from many of my worldly cares, even if only for a few minutes.

That is what it's not, but what is it?

Humility, and being humble, is outward centered, rather than inward centered. It looks at the needs, wants, and desires of others as well as your own. Modesty is also present. Modesty doesn't bring attention to oneself but lends itself to a more subtle, inner beauty that we all possess. Instead of puffing oneself up, the humble adopt a "lower" or lowly position, giving others more esteem than they give themselves. Humility also has at its foundation a sense of teachability or being coachable.

As you can see, gentle reader, humility is strangely lacking from our culture in the twenty-first century. Today, we seem to be more interested in "me" than in "you." We have become fixated on looking good and sounding good. The physical-enhancement industry has blossomed into a $16 billion industry in 2016. Now, there is nothing wrong with wanting to look better on the outside, but don't you think equal time and money should be given to developing the inside? One's inner beauty?

Anecdote time. This relates to pride and how deceived we can be about ourselves. It also offers some perspective on how others view us. Back in the eighties, when I was in my twenties and recently married, I would meet together with a man I respected and wanted to learn from. One evening, he came over for one of our bi-weekly chats, and I mentioned that I was struggling with pride (inner pride). His response has stuck with me for over thirty-five years, it was so profound. There were two parts to this profound response. After he picked himself off the floor from laughing so hard (the first part of his response), he simply asked, "What on earth do *you* have to be proud of?" (italics added). Okay, I may have embellished that just a tad. What really happened wasn't too far off, however. When I mentioned my pride issue(s), he quietly sat back in his chair, pondered what I said, and then, sincerely, asked the above question, without such an emphasis on "you."

Before I answered the question, an epiphany of wisdom hit me. That wisdom was simply, "Don't be too quick to answer this one." Why? Because the first thing that came to my mind was all my accomplishments to date. It struck me in that moment that he was asking me a spiritual question, and this deserved a spiritual response. It had nothing, or very little, to do with what I had done or was doing but rather had everything to do with my inner man: what I thought, how I felt, what issues and reactions I kept in, and which ones I let loose. And so began, as John and Paul (the Beatles, not the Apostles) so eloquently said, my journey down the "long and winding road."

Instead of going into great deal on the topic of humility, I am going to end it here. Don't get me wrong, I will not be leaving the topic "as is" but rather I will weave and speak about it throughout the book, such is the importance of this spiritual trait.

Points to Ponder

1. *Are there any areas in my life that are a source of negative pride?*

2. *On a scale of one to ten, how do I treat the needs of others: physical, emotional, and spiritual, in relation to my own needs?*

Chapter 7
FORGIVENESS

I will forgive others even as I have been forgiven

This spiritual characteristic is at the core of our human development. All of us have been offended, and all of us have offended someone else. Usually the offenders are loved ones, or at least, those closest to us. Those we offend are often the same ones. More on this a little later.

So, why is forgiveness, or the lack thereof, such an issue? Why don't we just move on? Well, you have undoubtedly heard of someone having "a lot of baggage." This baggage is made up of all the offenses that a person has experienced and hasn't dealt with, having left them unresolved and unforgiven. It also includes all the times that a person hurts or offends someone else. I liken this to a person wearing a backpack through life. As offenses occur, a new brick is added to the backpack. If we don't deal with the offense, the brick stays. As more offenses occur, more bricks are added. As you can see, our souls get weighed down with junk as we continue on with life. This happens without our even knowing it. For many of us, the backpacks are full, and we are walking around dragging our issues like boat anchors. Backpacks and boat anchors, what a combination. An oversimplification, perhaps, but illustrative nevertheless.

At the core of forgiveness is humility. Humility is at the core of forgiving and being forgiven. When forgiving someone, you are denying yourself, giving up your "right" to be offended, and pardoning the offending party. This is not an easy task, nor is it simple. It is, however, essential to living with a healthy and free spirit. Humility is essential when being forgiven, simply because we are usually confessing a wrong word or behavior that has hurt someone. Without humility, the words and actions of asking for forgiveness are empty and hollow.

Unforgiveness

When we harbor unforgiveness in our hearts, we are weighed down with the burden of the offenses that have been committed against us, or the ones we commit against others. What many of us don't realize is that we are also weighed down with not being forgiven. When we offend or hurt someone, it is imperative that we ask forgiveness. The air needs to be cleared between us. Our spirits know when there are issues between us, and this begins to burden us as we go on with our lives. If we walk around with unforgiven issues in our lives, we are just adding another brick to the backpack. It is like a wedge being driven between our minds and our souls, between us and those around us. We begin living in tension with ourselves and with others.

What exactly do I mean by the power of forgiveness? Remember the story about when I was working as an immigration officer at the Vancouver International Airport? The event was described earlier in the book, but what wasn't described was what happened a couple of years later. My wife invited a few friends over to pray for me, that my back would be healed. I had been in serious chronic pain for over two years, and there was no respite in sight. About halfway through the time of prayer, one of the girls asked me a delicate question. "Have you ever forgiven the guy involved?"

Wait, what? Me forgive him? No! What was I supposed to do? Offer forgiveness to someone who obviously didn't want nor care for my forgiveness? A guy who was intent on inflicting harm for his own selfish reasons, and who was successful, I might add. My mind was reeling. On the one hand, every breath I took reminded me of this guy; such is the nature of intense pain. I could still see his face. The hatred and bitterness were all I had to hold on to. There was a perverse sense of comfort present in it. In some twisted way, I had almost become friends with hatred and bitterness. On the other hand, I wanted to be free from the pain; I wanted to be free from allowing this guy to live rent free in my mind. Most importantly, I wanted to be free, albeit subconsciously, in my spirit from the baggage associated with this whole event.

This battle raged in my mind for an eternal five or six seconds. What I mean is, the mind can go through so many thoughts in so little time. It just seems like forever. It's like driving down the road and your mind starts to wander. A few seconds later, you come to and wonder what happened to the last mile or two. It doesn't take long; it just seems like forever. Such was the moment I was having with all the ramifications of forgiving this guy. It was an epic battle with the devil on one shoulder, spewing his lies, and an angel on the other shoulder, speaking words of comfort and truth. Like I said, after an eternal five or six seconds, I squeaked out a "No." It was a sheepish, almost inaudible "no." I didn't want to, but I knew better. Good grief, I had graduated from seminary, been to all kinds of inner-healing and personal-growth seminars. Even the secular seminars pounded home the concept of forgiveness. So, yeah, I knew better; I knew what had to be done, and what was expected of me.

My eyes fell to the floor as I braced for the next penetrating question. The girls were gracious. "Do you think you should?" they asked, as my eyes began to mysteriously leak copious amounts of fluid. They were both gracious and gentle, seeing my inner angst. The tears gave way to sobs as I began doing battle with myself. Make no mistake, the inner and outer pain that people deal with on a daily basis is significant, to say the least. So, I forgave him. Then I forgave him again, and again. The more I forgave him, the more the inner turmoil dissipated. I just kept repeating my forgiveness to myself, in my mind. I felt a spiritual release taking place. Ten years later, I am still forgiving him.

The long and short of this story is that, over the next little while, my body started to shed the stress caused by the burden of unforgiveness. My shoulders started to relax, and my intense neck spasms started to ease off. Same with my lower back. Things were getting manageable, and all because I took the simple step of forgiving someone who had caused me pain. Remarkable.

There is an old saying that goes, "We are most like animals when we fight, most like man when we judge, and most like God when we forgive." There certainly seems to be some divinely inspired inner activity when we forgive or ask for forgiveness.

In the spirit of "better late than never," allow me to give a definition of what forgiveness is and what it isn't. Let's start with what it isn't: Saying sorry is not forgiveness. It is being sorry. "Sorry" is not a verb. It is an adjective, describing one's feelings of sorrow, remorse, and regret. Being sorry is part of the whole forgiveness package. Being sorry alone can have some negative connotations. One can be sorry they got caught, or sorry for their behavior. An apology is similar to being sorry, although it has been said it is a more formal type of sorry. Implied in both these words is the concept of forgiveness, despite there being no forgiveness explicitly asked for nor explicitly given. In my humble opinion, I feel our culture is getting painfully close by giving "sorry" and "I apologize" the de facto meaning of forgiveness.

If we think of the offense as a debt, using banking terms, then forgiveness is the cancelling of said debt. When a debt gets cancelled, or forgiven, that's it. It's over. No more payments are required. For example, if you borrowed some money from someone, a large amount, and you were having a hard time paying it back, and you went to the lender and said you were sorry you ever took the loan out, he may nod his head with a small amount of empathy and then remind you when your next payment is due. If, however, you asked for some respite from the loan, he may actually offer to forgive the debt, eliminating it altogether. No more payments necessary. Not like that would ever happen in our banking culture, but I have heard it's okay to dream and fantasize.

Such is the nature of forgiveness. It is like the canceling of a debt—the debt, in this case, being an offense committed. Now, here's where things get tricky. If you are like the lender, or the one offended, the forgiveness process may take some time. You may find yourself forgiving on multiple occasions. Although the concept of forgiving is a fairly simple process, it is not an easy one. Some of the toughest things in life are found in the realm of forgiving someone for the hurt they have caused. If you want to experience inner wholeness, spiritual freedom and vitality, then forgive you must. Please note, gentle reader, this is not a suggestion. It is an essential part of the wholesome and free spiritual life that is available to each of us.

I would be remiss if I didn't address more fully the whole concept of asking for forgiveness. No one has gone through life without offending someone in some way. In order to experience spiritual peace, we need to clean the slate. We do this by asking forgiveness and making amends. Making amends is essential in spiritual wholeness and peace. It is so important that it is included as step ten in the twelve steps of Alcoholics Anonymous.

Asking forgiveness and making amends is a skill I have become comfortable with, much to my everlasting chagrin. Myriad are the people whom I have offended over the course of my life. Oddly enough, the number of people I have offended is very close to the number of people I have had to make amends with and ask for forgiveness. What I have found in my experience is that when I am confronted with an offense, depending on the severity of said offense, I will take a moment, ponder the issue, allow what is said to sink in (at this time, I will mentally go through what I remember of the situation, to get context), get a feel for the pain and sincerity of the offended person, and then repeat back to them as verbatim as possible what I heard them say. It goes something like this, "So what I hear you saying is when I did/said whatever it was, that you felt offended by (the specific thing I did). I am so sorry that I did that. I apologize. Would you forgive me for.... (whatever it was)?" The key to the whole enterprise is to be sincere in your delivery, not dismissive or flippant. Remember the definition of "sorry?" Ya gotta *be* sorry if you're gonna *say* sorry.

I find this little formula covers the bases, so to speak, emotionally— from my perspective, at least. I express remorse, regret, and give them an opportunity to forgive me, as much as they can at the time. I understand that it may be a process, again depending on the severity of the offense. I also realize that they may not be prepared to offer forgiveness at this point.

This brings up another point. Let's say they did not bring it up, and I felt convicted of my bad behavior toward them. If I ask for forgiveness and it is not forthcoming, what do I do? If I have sincerely gone through the process, that is all I can do; the rest is up to them. I need to respect their process of forgiving, accept their position, and move on. I am *not* responsible for being forgiven. I can't control the outcome, as much as I would like to, even though I may feel as though I need to. Me being forgiven is *not up to me*. My role is confessing my offense, apologizing, making amends, and asking forgiveness. Full stop. That is what I am in control of. Not receiving forgiveness when asked to be forgiven is tough; make no mistake about it. It takes discipline to move on from that; so feel free to go through the process, feel the pain, and move on.

It goes without saying that, over the past ten years, I have offended many friends and family with my addiction issues. Unfortunately, I have yet to fully clear the slate with everyone. Most, but there are still some stragglers out there. Not that they are straggling; I just haven't gotten to them yet.

Points to Ponder

1. *Who have I hurt and need to ask forgiveness from?*

2. *Who has hurt me who I need to forgive?*

3. *What, if anything, is holding me back from asking for forgiveness or from forgiving?*

4. *Is the weight of forgiveness, whether given or asked for, worth not acting on it?*

Chapter 8
PEACE

If you Google the word "peace," you will find a number of definitions referring to the absence of conflict, be it internationally or interpersonally. There is an implied concept of personal tranquility but nothing explicit. I want to explore the concept of inner, soul peace, the type of peace that allows you to be okay with you.

Included in the concept of peace is the ability to rest. Often, our lives get so busy, whether by necessity or self-inflicted busy-ness, that we are unable to truly come to a state of rest. We will try everything to achieve this, from sleeping pills, relaxants in the form of Benzodiazepines, better mattresses for our beds, better pillows, better sheets, and the list goes on. Granted, there may be some who are in need of some physical changes to their sleeping arrangements, but for the most part, these are temporary fixes.

We will try anything to find this elusive rest—anything that doesn't involve doing any personal, inner work to eliminate the inner angst that keeps us from experiencing true rest, true peace. The operative word here is "work." Make no mistake, dealing with all your baggage and personal junk is going to take no small amount of blood, sweat, and tears. What may not have seemed so bad way back when it happened will have inevitably grown into a massive, gangrenous cesspool of toxic ooze, unrecognizable to the human eye. Know this, gentle reader, you owe it to yourself to deal with this excrement that is growing and festering under the surface of the bold façade you have erected.

Let's revisit the loaded backpack for a moment. Let's assume for a moment that each brick is the source of inner angst, causing stress, either consciously or subconsciously. Just as the bricks would weigh us down physically, the spiritual bricks weigh our spirits down. This is manifest in anger, shortness of temper, impatience, becoming rushed, having little grace for others, and self-centeredness. Walls go up, doors are slammed shut, and windows are boarded. Nothing and no one will be allowed into to our innermost selves. We will rarely, if ever, open up to anyone. Such is the nature of stress and pain in our lives.

One of the issues mentioned above is self-centeredness. We go into protection mode, not wanting to be hurt again. We definitely seek to limit and mitigate any pain that comes our way. Our defenses are at the ready to fend off any and all attacks against us. It is like the only tool in our tool kit is a hammer, and therefore, every problem becomes a nail, and we will beat that nail into submission every chance we get. The golden rule becomes, "Do unto others *before* they do unto you." The amount of hurt and pain we have experienced will determine the amount of retaliation and/or attack, either internal or external, we offer in response. It is this reaction to hurt and pain that leads to anxiety and depression, telling ourselves all kinds of lies and acting accordingly. The way we act out our pain is learned behavior. We can just as easily—well, maybe not just as easily—unlearn it and replace it with responsible, loving, and kind behavior. We can say no to the lies and start believing the truth about ourselves.

Pain and the unforgiveness of the causes of pain will lead to one of the biggest and vilest enemies of our spirits and spiritual life: isolation. When we experience emotional pain and suffering, we tend to handle it much the same way we handle physical trauma. When we experience physical trauma, in the form of accidents or surgery or whatever, we tend to go into "recovery" mode. For example, I recently had surgery to remove an epigastric hernia. The suggestion by the surgeon was to remain in bed and rest for a few hours, then take it very easy for some time, not doing any strenuous activity. Since it was an outpatient procedure, I was able to be fairly mobile fairly quickly. The point is, the more intense the procedure, the more intense the recovery period, the longer we remain bedridden. Generally speaking, this time of recovery is done alone, or at least with close family or loved ones close by. We do the same with emotional trauma. We become bedridden, curl up on the sofa with a blanky and binge watch Netflix. An afternoon alone turns into a couple of days, which turns into a week, then a month, and then…. People begin to wonder if we are still alive.

As a coincidental aside, isolation is the friend of the drug addict. I am not talking about party drugs, but heroin. This drug is usually done alone or with another trusted user or two. It is not something we do in the living room with our "normal" parents or siblings with us. It is not a party drug. We isolate to hide the cold hard truth that we are dependent on a substance for physical sustenance.

Back to being hurt and self-centered. This will often lead to the inner "tapes" being played on the speakers of our minds. We all have experienced the evils of listening to this streaming service, after all, it's free. You know the ones; they are the words that tell us we are not worthy of … anything, that we are pathetic, that we will fail, why bother, et cetera.

Along these lines, we should get in the habit of speaking words of truth and inspiration over our lives. This is another arrow in the quiver of establishing peace in our spirits. This will seem very awkward initially, but hang in there, it is so worth it. Plus, it beats the other stuff, the curses we speak over our lives. Start blessing yourself with words that will bring life instead of death.

Another word that accompanies peace is the word harmony. *Dictionary. com* defines harmony as "agreement; accord; harmonious relations; a consistent, orderly, or pleasing arrangement of parts; congruity." This definition, though worthy, just doesn't seem to do justice to such a lovely sounding word. It seems like such a forensic definition. A "pleasing arrangements of parts" starts to do it justice. At least the point is made. If we extend this into the realm of music, when a number of voices and/or instruments are working in harmony, a marvelous and wonderful sound emanates. The same can be said about food and smells and tastes. When colors are blended, we can see magnificent kaleidoscopes.

When we live in harmony with others and with ourselves, it is also a thing of beauty. Our lives and relationships become a kaleidoscope of beauty, harmony, and peace. Of course, with this harmony comes no small amount of inner peace. The question is this: Why do we not seek to live in peace and harmony with others? If it is such a wonderful thing, why do we avoid it and even fight it? It seems we prefer to allow people to live rent free in our minds rather than serving them with an eviction notice, or at least, making peace with them so we can all live in harmony. Then there is the victim-mentality mindset that I will get into later. Often, we validate our lives by living as victims and giving control over to others.

Along with getting along with others, living in peace also means getting along with ourselves. Every one of us needs to go through a process of personal reconciliation. Some would call it forgiving yourself. I am not a fan of that concept. I am not sure you can fully forgive yourself. You can, however, cut yourself some slack and give yourself a break with respect to carrying the offense any longer.

There is another aspect of inner peace that I would like to address. That is the whole concept of expectations. I have found, in my humble experience, that the higher the expectation, the higher the risk for disappointment if the expectation is not met. I speak from the experience of not living up to or meeting expectations. Yes, I have been the cause of considerable disappointment for those associated with me. So, I am speaking from personal experience on the other side of the expectation/disappointment equation.

With this in mind, suffice to say that I do my best not to expect much, if anything, from anyone. If things happen as planned, then all is well. I am pleasantly surprised. If they don't, I wasn't expecting them to anyway, so no big deal. So, yes, I make plans and organize my life. No, I don't bet the ranch expecting these plans to all come to fruition.

The flip side to this is that, when I give my word to someone, telling them I will do something, then come hell or high water, I will do it. Of course, this is the post-addiction me speaking. I do not want to be the cause of someone's inner angst at my failure or inability to complete something. My actions have disappointed enough people; I don't want to perpetuate that legacy.

What I have found to be very helpful has been the thought that, win, lose, or draw, I am going to be a decent human. By doing good and right, I have found that peace transcends my situations and permeates my soul. Being at peace with myself and with others, to me, seems to be one of life's highest callings. Please note: It does not mean compromising my morals or principles. It simply means that I am not going to fight every battle that presents itself before me. It means letting go of things and not taking them so personally.

Although there is more that can be said about peace, I am going to end it here, but will likely touch on it in future chapters.

Points to Ponder

1. *How is peace stolen from me?*

2. *What expectations do I place on myself and others?*

3. *Are these expectations too high? Am I being reasonable?*

4. *How can I best handle disappointment so as not to lose my peace?*

Chapter 9
AWARENESS

I find that awareness is like the missing link in one's emotional, spiritual walk. I lived most of my life in a state of being self-absorbed, egotistical, and selfish, unaware of how my actions affected the lives of others. Of course, my actions were rarely inspiring, which would mean that it looked as though I actually cared for others. Silly me. The world revolved around me and was in place to meet my needs. Why on earth would I care how anyone else felt? Not the sharpest bulb in the shed, or something like that.

The transition went something like this to begin with: When I was young and single, I had all the answers, and wasn't afraid to voice my opinion. When I got married, I realized that I didn't have quite all the answers and kept some of my opinions to myself. When I had kids and they became teenagers, I realized I didn't even know the questions and just kept my mouth shut. Now I am far more flexible in life, leading a quiet life of observation and adaptation. Don't get me wrong; I'm not some wishy-washy man whose mind changes day to day, like the proverbial cork in the ocean being tossed to and fro. These days I am slow to speak, sensitive to the needs of others, and living by the golden rule of doing unto others as I would have them do unto me. A lot of times people just want you to listen; you don't need all the right things to say, and chances are that you don't have the right answer. After all, God gave us two ears and one mouth, so we should learn to use them proportionally.

Another issue I found I was lacking in was my awareness of my own feelings, let alone the feelings of others. I did find, however, that when I became aware of my own feelings, I could more easily relate with others. The hard part was admitting that I even had feelings and emotions and that they could be hurt. But when I finally became aware of myself, back in my mid to late thirties, the flood of tears and emotion actually scared people. But what a relief. All those years of pent-up emotion stuffed down under a hardened shell of tough, macho intimidation made for a spectacle of biblical proportions. Whoa! Epic, indeed.

The benefits of all this emotional awareness were a renewed marriage, I became a better employee, and my kids finally got a father figure they could love and respect before it was too late for them. Oddly enough, none of those benefitted me directly. I mean, who wouldn't want to be easier to live with, to work with, to just be around without feeling judged or criticized or intimidated or inferior? But not me; I had no problems … not. Anyway, the journey of awareness is fraught with bumps, ditches, and potholes. It's not all clear sailing, though there are moments of calmness and peace. The good news is these moments get longer and occur with greater frequency.

Then comes the "adaptation" issue. Translated, this means change. For me, this was a big deal. It's not that I resisted change; it was the growing pains. I went from being a complete rectal sphincter to being a fairly normal, regular guy. Believe me, the change was epic, not to mention painful. Just ask my wife and kids. From being a completely self-absorbed putz, I became a fairly giving, sensitive, even inspiring man (not my words, by the way). My point, and I have one, is that change—spiritually induced change—is a life transforming, blessed event that your love ones will be eternally grateful for.

Change, for the most part, usually comes in bite-sized morsels. In many cases, it is barely noticeable in the short term. Have faith; it is occurring. Looking back over the weeks and months, you will definitely see marked differences in your behavior; even your thinking and thought processes will be different, more mature.

And then there is getting along with others. Sometimes that can seem more trouble than it's worth, but it is worth it. Living in peace and harmony takes work. By work, I mean work, discipline, and thoughtfulness. It is a constant process that seems to bring more stress on our lives than what we are prepared to endure. Endure it anyway. If we all give up on one another, we begin to live in a pit of despair, and no one is happy. We can bring some happiness and joy and peace to those around us. Let's be purveyors of good in our world, and ultimately, the world will thank us.

Awareness is the product of contrition and humility. It is said that awareness of your problem is the beginning of the healing process. After all, why would we need healing if we think nothing is wrong? This is especially true in the world of addiction. Personally, I lived in denial of my addiction to pain meds. What was obvious to those closest to me, I completely and totally denied. Then I lost my job, my wife and daughter left, the house left, my truck left without me, and I was left with nothing, except the lie that I was okay. What solace. This went on for years. Drug usage that went from prescription pain meds to street drugs, from "snorting" to IV usage. From opiates only to adding crystal meth. Why? Because I could. Did I mention all my good friends left? Gone. I was pitched out like last week's garbage. Yes, it was me who was behaving like last week's garbage, the smell becoming so unbearable that I was shunned by pretty much everyone. But that was their issue, not mine. Or so I told myself.

As the years went by, I kept trying to get free from the disease that had infected me. Let me say from the outset that what started as a conscious choice soon morphed into a full-on sickness. I wanted so much to get out of the life that had so consumed me but couldn't, or perhaps, wouldn't would be more accurate. Towards the end of my addicted lie, I mean, life, I remember saying to my son and his girlfriend, who I was living and using with, that we should all get off the stuff and act as our own support group. This came after a two-month stint in a recovery center. I had been clean for a few months, but there was no support system in place for me. I was still shunned by everyone and all alone. So, what did I do? I self-destructed and went back to what I had come to know: drugs. Some leader.

This went on for another two years. It finally came to an end when my son and his girlfriend got pregnant and my first grandson was born. I am sure you remember this from the beginning of the book, where the birth of the child was my catalyst for getting back into detox. After completing my detox time, I signed up for the same recovery place as I had attended three years previously.

As fate would have it, I saw the lady there whom I totally bonded with. What had happened was that my funding had fallen through, and I was only there one day and night. As I was sitting in the lobby getting ready to leave, she sat down next to me and asked if she could speak frankly to me. "Of course," I replied. She began by saying that when I was there last, I was the picture of health and vitality, both physically and psychologically/emotionally. If anyone was going to succeed "in the real world" it was me. Or so all the staff thought. "So, what happened?" she asked. I was at a loss, which is odd for me. But given what was happening to me on the inside at that very moment, the "being at a loss" was no surprise. It seemed as though God was "downloading" everything I had learned and experienced during my stay there, those three years prior. Not only that, but I was feeling a strange resolve, a powerful force welling up within my spirit and soul that this was the end of the addiction lifestyle. It took me awhile, but I soon realized that this was a God thing. Once again, it is interesting to note that God is mentioned a total of six times in the Alcoholic Anonymous twelve steps. It certainly seemed as though I was having a "moment" with my higher power. Perhaps he wasn't done with me just yet.

What was interesting was that, although I had been inspired to write this book while at Pacifica and had banged off a complete outline, all I had was an outline written in long hand, cursive script. Nothing else, nada, niente. I had nothing else until that moment. That was when everything fell into place for me. Well, most everything. I still needed something into which to input all my thoughts, like a nice computer, specifically a MacBook Air or Pro would be nice. As fate would have it, I had to wait six months before I got my iPad Pro with a Bluetooth folio. Not too shabby. Four months after getting my iPad, the book was done. A week and a half after that, I was on page sixty of my second book. As my sainted mother would not hesitate to tell me, "The Lord works in mysterious ways, His wonders to perform." Amen, Mom. She also incessantly told me that, "All things work together for good, to those who love God, who are called according to His purpose." Digressing, once again. Let me get back on topic.

The interesting part of that anecdote is that I had been waiting since 1994—the year I decided that I wanted to write a book but didn't know what to write about—and had nothing, whatsoever until 2014. Twenty years in the wilderness, wandering aimlessly, barely getting by. What I wasn't aware of was that it became painfully evident that God was preparing me, deep within my soul and spirit, as I "wandered" through my desert, through my *dark night of the soul*. During that time, I had my greatest growth, becoming aware, for the first time, of what I had become (not cool), of who God had actually created me to be, and that there were some seriously rough edges to knock off on my spiritual journey. Further to this, I became very aware (real cool) of who God really was/is in my life and who He was/is in the world.

Most of these edges almost came off naturally, as in I dealt with them as I became aware of them. This didn't make it any less painful to go through the process, but it did make life less burdened—less burdened for me, my loved ones, and those who I came into contact with on a daily basis. I mean, picture if you will some big guy, full of unrequited anger, carry a massive backpack that was filled with bricks, who was going through life swinging a razor-sharp scythe, slicing and dicing anyone and anything that he came in contact with. That was me from the age of fifteen, when I was going through full-onset hormonal adolescent rage until the age of thirty-seven and a half (yes, and a half). That was the age when I attended for the first time a personal-growth, inner-healing seminar called "Choices, the Adventure of a Lifetime." It was led by a woman from Texas (being a Baylor alum, I instantly related) named Thelma Box, who at one time had a partner named Phil McGraw, or Dr. Phil. Anyway, this five-day seminar was the catalyst I needed to open the eyes of my heart and see inside. To see what everyone else was seeing and experiencing, which really wasn't very good at all. I was devastated. The only thing that saved me was the whirlwind nature of the seminar, which knocked you (your awareness) down and built you back up. During the seminar, I didn't necessarily want to *kill* the leaders, or training assistants (TAs), but I did want to inflict serious and grievous bodily injury to them.

During the "knock down" phase, I found myself asking if this was all true. Needless to say, I didn't sleep much the four nights in attendance. I was far too busy dealing with all my issues. The TAs were cold-blooded and ruthless, and it wasn't until the final day of the seminar that I realized that the TAs were actually quite pained, acting out their little cold-blooded charade, and were actually very loving, very healed in their approach, realizing that their approach was what was needed in almost all cases, especially mine.

Anyway, the things that I dealt with were both legion (many) and epic. The awareness that I experienced was, to say the least, life altering, radically life altering. So often, awareness is like that when it comes to ourselves. Many times in my life, I felt like the guy I mentioned earlier, the one who was waiting for God to save him from the flood. I realized much later that God had provided every opportunity for me to change my behavior, to become a more humble, wiser, quieter man. But no, I wasn't listening; I was too busy talking. It took a hardcore seminar to "jerk the slack" right out of me.

There is an old story, totally fictitious, about a guy who was living alone when a damn broke, and the flood waters were coming. He asked God to save him and was convinced that God would, in fact, do just that. As the water reached his property, guys in a jeep came by to rescue him. He refused, saying God would save him. Before long, the water was up to his porch, and some guys in a boat came by to save him. Nope, God would save him. Inevitably, the water rose so much that our man was stuck on his roof when a helicopter came by to rescue him. Go away; God would save him. The water rose even further, washing him away to his ultimate and final demise. When he got to heaven, he asked God what happened, having been convinced that God would save him. God replied that on three separate occasions he had sent someone by to rescue him. Such is the power of awareness.

Like the guy in the flood, I experience death that weekend. Death to myself in many ways, death to the way I experienced life, to the way I interacted with people, to the way I interacted with God and even myself. There was only one more ugly issue that was hidden deep beneath the surface, and that was the issue of addiction that may have been caused by the sexual abuse I experienced as a child. Talk about dealing with deep issues. I became aware of the abject ugliness of my life, becoming aware of the complete depravity of my soul and my complete and total reliance on God. This is incredibly humbling, having to go through these lessons at my age.

I do things so backwards. Where most people "sow their wild oats" when they are young and learn and grow in life as they get older, I seemed to follow the "Benjamin Button syndrome" of starting off life reasonably good, getting better, then falling precipitously before experiencing redemption. The fact that there were waves, cresting and troughing, through good and bad, is a testament to God's grace in my life. There have been times in my life where I have thought that

free will really sucks. These are usually at the times of my greatest experiences of awareness (and by greatest, I mean worst), although they can be looked at as being the best in the long run. Once again, looking at life through spiritual eyes, it becomes clear that God's hand was always on me, never leaving, never giving up, always faithfully by my side. Of this, I am fully aware.

Points to Ponder

1. *What is my situational awareness?*

2. *Am I aware of the effects that my words and actions are having on others?*

3. *How can I become more aware? (see "Mindfulness" chapter)*

Chapter 10
WISDOM AND KNOWLEDGE

I will be in a constant state of learning and
absorbing wisdom and knowledge, shunning
arrogance and embracing humility.

One of the key attributes for successful, peaceful living is humility. If "love" is
a foundation for life, then "humility" is a foundation for love. I am speaking
of a spiritual type of love in this instance, not an erotic, lustful, self-serving,
self-gratifying, "what's in it for me" type of love. Spiritual love is giving,
other-serving, not looking out only for its own interests but for the interests
of others. It doesn't look at what it can get, but what it can give. At the root
of all of this is humility. I am not talking about a weak, milquetoast state
of being, but rather an inner strength that overcomes the spinelessness that
seems so prevalent in our modern culture.

Humility, in this case, has us realize that we don't know it all and there is
much learning and wisdom to glean from life that we don't already have. Life
becomes a classroom, and life's lessons become endless sources of learning
experiences. The funny thing is that, the more we learn, the more we don't
know, and the more we need to learn. If learning wasn't so much fun, it
would be a vicious cycle of chasing one's tail. This seems to parallel my life
quite significantly. As I've said before, when I was a young person, I knew it
all and arrogantly let everyone know that I knew it all. Falling in love and
getting married, I quickly realized that I didn't have all the answers. Then,

when I had kids and they became teenagers, I quickly realized that I didn't even know the questions, let alone the answers.

It would seem that the antithesis of humility is arrogance, self-aggrandizement, selfishness, and boastfulness. Although I struggled with being boastful, arrogance was second nature to me. I cleverly disguised this arrogance as self-confidence. Unfortunately for me, or fortunately as the case may be, I could only keep this façade up for so long. It was much easier with friends, because we moved quite a lot and friends changed. My wife, however, has been in my life going on four decades. Being exceptionally intuitive, I didn't really fool her for very long. Actually, she is also very spiritually in tune, so nothing got by her for long.

My arrogance knew no bounds; I believed and acted as though the world revolved around me, the center of my own little universe. It's a good thing that we moved around so much. The moving stopped in my early thirties, and we have been living in the same community for thirty years. Maintaining my arrogance-disguised-as-self-confidence ruse was destined for an early burial. It lasted eleven years into my marriage, before I started doing some personal work, some inner healing, as it were.

One of the areas in my life that was the hardest to leave behind was my humor. It's not that I became some humorless automaton, but I had always hidden behind my humor, using it as a mask to hide behind. This was a product of my upbringing. Moving so often, I found that I "had to" excel in sports and congeniality in order to be accepted. After all, who knew when we would be moving and leaving all these new-found friends? Well, the sports and humor followed me through life, the humor developing into a form-fitting mask that would make the creators of *Mission Impossible* proud, hiding my inner self. With the advent of knowledge and wisdom in my life, through my journey into inner healing and self-awareness, I realized that I didn't need to be funny to be accepted. I simply needed to be real and honest. To coin a current buzzword, I needed to be "authentic," which is a big word for "real." I also needed to be real in a socially acceptable manner. No point in being a real jerk, after all. Being aware of my thoughts, words, and actions was the beginning a long and fruitful process. Don't get me wrong; I have by no means arrived and catch myself on a daily basis reverting to bad habits like losing my temper, and consequently, my words betray me.

Awareness virtually gob-smacked me in right in the face, right between the eyes. The eyes of my heart were opened for the first time since the age of ten, the same year, oddly enough, that I was sexually abused by an older cousin. Amazing what the mind will do to protect itself from pain, or even the fear of pain. Add excelling at sports into the mix, and I had the perfect storm for a full-blown dysfunction of arrogance to deal with. It was through oceans of tears that I finally saw myself for who I was, who I could/should be, and who, come "hell or high water," I was determined to become.

I would love to tell you that clear sailing was my experience on my new voyage. But I was totally committed to my "trip," and there were days, even weeks and months, that were fraught with tears, tears, and more tears.

As I began to become more spiritually aware in my everyday life, I began to notice small changes in my behavior and even my thought process. I began to slow down my response time in conversations, actually pondering what was being said to me. Even listening intently. Wow, listening to others, what a novel concept. I wanted my life to be congruent with my belief system and not the other way around. Call me crazy, but when I talked with God, I kinda thought He should be listening to me—that He would, in fact, be listening to me. Could I do any less to people speaking to me? Could I do any less with God, believing He would actually talk with me and I should be listening? This was a novel experience for me: having my world revolve around others and not the other way around. It was then that I actually started empathizing with others, sharing in their experiences. Before long, I became quite a good listener; people started calling me to talk. Weird.

As I began spending more time becoming spiritually aware, life started changing even faster and with greater intensity. I was coaching women's volleyball at a local major university when one day, during a team dilemma, the head coach (I was an assistant) said to me, "T, I really need your wisdom on this." Another gob smack right between the eyes. "My wisdom?" You've got to be kidding me. The only thing that wisdom and I have in common is the letter "W." It is funny how others will notice the change in your life long before you are even aware you are changing.

Such is the case with wisdom. Humility is also at the root of wisdom. Simple math, actually: $1+2=2+1$. I learned that in grade nine or ten, I think. The commutative principle, I believe, if my memory serves. But I digress.

Wisdom plus humility equals humility plus wisdom. There is actually NO room for arrogance in living spiritually. Really, what do we bring to the table? Fortunately, since becoming more and more aware of my inner condition, such as it was, the "gob smack" incidents became farther and fewer between. The interesting thing is that they were laced with such grace that the level of intensity was so much more manageable.

The spiritual life is so gentle with those who have a willing heart (as opposed to those who are in open and wanton rebellion). It may be hard to believe, but there is enough love in the world for each and every one of us. Our problem is that we seem to choose to wallow in self-pity and victimhood. Surely, we can't be worthy of any deep and abiding love. I mean, how many of us think that what we've done in life is so bad that, surely, we can't be forgiven for it? Surely, we can't be part of the "none," whom I mentioned earlier. Like you're the only one in history. Right.

It's like they say in the cop shows: "We can do this the easy way or the hard way." The easy way is to simply realize that forgiveness is a matter of asking for it, receiving it, and walking in it. We get hung up on the receiving part, which is simply a matter of believing that there are those who want to forgive us, and that this forgiveness can actually lead to a full pardon of all our evil deeds, past, present, and future. If we believe it, then we need to walk it. And so, we begin down the path of wisdom.

As like all disciplines, walking in wisdom takes discipline. Another novel concept. It almost seems to be a "chicken and egg" thing. Does learning and knowledge come before wisdom or vice versa? And, of course, does wisdom come before humility, or is that the other way around? Personally, I say, "Who cares?" As long as both are present, it's a win/win. Maybe if we were talking about the evolutionary process, the "chicken/egg" question would have some relevance, but again, I digress.

The bottom line in this whole discussion is that true, spiritual humility is one of the foundational keys to a better life. It also allows us to learn more about life: who we are, where we are going, and where we fit, and just as important, it allows us to acknowledge what we DON'T know, and to be okay with that. The key to knowledge is learning from our experiences, especially our bad decisions or experiences. What is retained from these experiences is the basis, or foundation, for wisdom. Where wisdom shines is in the application in our daily lives of the experiences we have endured. Remember, it is the incredible pressure we endure in life that produces some of the most beautiful diamonds of our personal history.

Points to Ponder

1. *What were some of the more difficult experiences in your life?*

2. *How could you have done things differently, either to avoid the problem altogether or how you reacted to said problem?*

3. *What are some of the greatest lessons you have learned in life?*

4. *How have you appropriated these lessons as instruments of inner growth?*

Chapter 11
GIVING IT AWAY

I will not keep Wisdom and Learning
to myself. I will give it away.

One of the things I have learned over the years is that people don't care how much you know until they know how much you care. Yes, it is a cliché but fairly poignant. Talk comes cheap, and in today's soundbite society, everyone has an opinion and somehow feels obligated to share, whether it is wanted or solicited. I know most of the things people say to me, the advice they give me, can be easily categorized as gibberish. They don't really care about me or my well-being; they just care about hearing themselves speak, the sound of their own voices waxing melodic in their auditory canals.

There is a proper time to share, and that would be easily described as when one has built sufficient emotional/spiritual equity in the life of another. By this I mean that the person concerned feels safe enough in their relationship to seek out some advice and believe they can be of assistance. By the same token, if we see someone who could benefit from our experience, wisdom, or knowledge, and we have developed sufficient equity in their lives, we shouldn't hesitate to ask if we can be of assistance. When asking, however, we should be prepared for the somewhat inevitable rebuff—that is, being told "no;" they down want or need our input. Don't feel bad. The seed to your availability has been sown. It may be only a matter of time before they come to you asking your advice.

Let's move on. Any wisdom that we gain is usually a byproduct of our experience in life or any knowledge that we may have gained on our journey through life. There are a couple of different types of wisdom available. For the most part, one is theoretical, and one is practical; one looks at the nature of things, while the other is more interested in the results of an issue. Both are valuable in our discussion here.

It would almost seem as though wisdom is the "sum" or end result of the lessons learned from our experiences. One thing is certain: Wisdom does not develop in a vacuum. It's not genetic; we are not born with it. We don't have our mom or dad's wisdom. They had to develop it for themselves through the school of hard knocks, or any other school, for that matter. The issue is how open we are to learning from what we have experienced. Indeed, how open we are to learn from our parents: the good, the bad, and the ugly of what they have experienced. Or how about from the lessons that others can teach us? Wisdom would dictate that we take advantage of every experience/lesson that we come across in our lives. There is no end to the amount of learning that can be achieved with this type of mindset.

A couple of anecdotes are in order: There was a story going around some time ago about two brothers who were raised by an abusive mother. I don't know if it is true or not, so no need to fact check. She would often lock them in the dark crawl space under the stairs and leave them there all day, living in darkness with the rats and other vermin. It was a fairly traumatic experience, sometimes being locked there for days on end. As fate would have it, they both grew up and went their separate ways. The first brother went to be a successful (?) drug addict and criminal, always getting in trouble, living off the system, exploiting whoever and whatever he could. The second brother, on the other hand, studied hard, went to school, university, med school, and specialized in neurosurgery, becoming renowned in his field. Fate didn't end the story there. When a reporter was doing a feature on the doctor, he found out that he had a brother, looked him up, and did an interview. In one part of the interview, the reporter asked, "What happened?" The brother replied, "I was abused as a child, beaten, locked in a dark and depressing crawlspace with rats and wasn't fed very often. What choice did I have?"

Armed with this information, the reporter went back to the doctor and asked about his upbringing. The doctor replied, "I was abused as a child, beaten, locked in a dark and depressing crawlspace with rats and wasn't fed very often. What choice did I have?" What choice indeed. Life is like that: Play the hand you're given or get out of the game. The key is to be able to see the hand for what it is, regardless of what it looks like.

For example, I am currently getting major dental work done and have had all my top teeth extracted. While at the dentist, I was asked how it was going. I thought for a second, and replied, "Well, with so few teeth, I don't go through near the toothpaste that I used to. Not only that, but not being able to chew very well has resulted in some much-needed weight loss." The girl was shocked by my positive attitude, saying, "Wow, most people don't see the positive and only complain when they're in here." Hmmm. Don't get me wrong; it wasn't too long ago that I would have been one of the whiners myself. But why complain and drag others down with you. Like my dear old dad used to say, "Smile, and the world smiles with you. Cry, and you cry alone." My question is this: Why not smile at adversity, indeed, laugh in its face, rather than piss and moan your way into isolation and oblivion? There is so much to be gained by being positive, and so much to lose by being negative. Choose being positive. NOTE: Being positive does not, in any way, mean living in denial. For example, it sucks being toothless. People look at me funny, and I'm sure they judge me, often thinking I'm some homeless derelict/drug addict. Little do they know that I had all my teeth when I was a homeless drug addict. So there. Of course, I started losing my teeth toward the end of my drug-addiction tenure, one of the consequences to an abusive lifestyle. Dental work sucks, pun intended. The point is, positivity and joy are things to be given away, not hoarded. It is just as easy to be positive and joyful as it is to be negative and cantankerous.

So where does that leave you? If you saw some toothless guy on the street, what would you think? Would there be any judgment? Would you steer clear of said toothless guy, fearing he would start begging for money, or worse? What does wisdom say? Let alone understanding, love, and compassion for our fellow man? Fortunately, I'm at the stage in my life where I know who I am, where I've come from, and where I'm going. Wisdom dictates to me that I don't judge others, regardless of how they look at me. Further, wisdom dictates that I don't judge other toothless, scabby, homeless, drug addicts, for once such was I (though not scabby).

Another story, this time from the bible: In the book of Genesis, we read the story of Joseph, who went from favored son, to abandoned and left for dead brother, to slave, to trusted employee, to framed employee, to prisoner, to dream interpreter, to the most revered and trusted man in Egypt, second only to Pharaoh. As the story goes, Joseph interpreted Pharaoh's dream, was made the number two in command of all Egypt, and wisely counseled Pharaoh on how best to handle the upcoming famine. So wise was his counsel that his fame traveled far and wide and ended up in the ears of his estranged father and brothers, who were sent by Dad to Egypt to buy some grain for the people under his care. Had Joseph acted irrationally, he likely would have squandered the grain supply, and there would have been none left for his family. Redemption for Israel would have had to find another way, if it were to be found at all.

I would be remiss not speaking of King Solomon in a discussion about wisdom. There is a story about one of his first tests as a new king: It is about two women and a baby. As the story goes, both women were brought to him claiming they each were the child's mother, each wanting the child for themselves. Solomon listened to their stories and rendered a decision: He ordered to child to be cut in half and each half given to one of the women. Real bright. But the story doesn't end there, it just begins. You see, it was the response of the women that told Solomon who the birth mother was. One of the women thought that this would be a great idea; chop the kid in half, and she would take her half home. The other woman, on the other hand, thought this was deplorable, and out of compassion and true motherly love, said that the other woman could have the whole, living baby, sparing the child's life. This was the response that Solomon was looking for, and he gave her the child, stating that only an imposter would rather see the child die and only a true mother would sacrifice possession of the child for the child's life.

The next question then becomes, "What do we do with this knowledge/ wisdom once we get it?" Once again, wisdom would dictate that we give it away at every opportunity. There is no point in hoarding it; we get no extra points when we die for the amount of wisdom we have kept for ourselves. In fact, if one were to believe in the divine afterlife, it would be a scary thought meeting God to give an account of our lives, knowing that we kept all the knowledge and wisdom to ourselves in a true act of selfishness (read: stupidity). Back to the original question: What to do with what we have? A simple principle of nature is reaping what you sow. That is to say, if the seeds of wisdom that you sow sparingly come back to you sparingly, don't be surprised. If, however, you sow abundantly, it is reasonable to be blessed with an abundant harvest; in this case, you will "harvest" even more wisdom. To "get" more, you need to give more away. It's that simple.

One of the keys to wisdom is that we, figuratively, stand on solid ground when we seek wisdom. Although this seems to fly in the face of faith, which is being certain of things unseen, it only seems that way. There is something about faith that brings out the best in people. Perhaps it's humility.

A last word on wisdom: It can come from the darkest, direst situations and experiences imaginable. It seems that the darker and direr the situation, the deeper the experience, the more intense the lessons learned, and of course, the more wisdom that is gained. A key element that I have not mentioned as yet is that of humility. Humility is the missing link, if you will, of what I have being saying about wisdom. Without it, your version of wisdom becomes nothing more than pop culture. People pontificating proudly, quite frankly, are a dime a dozen. The very heart of wisdom is humility. Oftentimes, the humble don't even realize that they are really quite wise and have much to share. Solomon said, "When pride comes, then comes shame; but with the lowly is wisdom." And "Pride goes before destruction…" and again, "A man's pride shall bring him low, but honor shall uphold the humble in spirit." Some pretty profound words from a pretty profound guy. Humility is the antithesis of pride and arrogance and selfishness. At the root of these positive virtues and blessing is humility.

One more thing to mention regarding the gaining of wisdom through the lessons we learn from our experiences in life: The enemy of wisdom gained from our experiences is when we adopt a victim mentality, when we feel hurt and offended and take these pains with us to justify our woeful experience in life. We allow these pains to then control us, and we relinquish our joy and peace and emotional wellbeing over to the experience or person responsible for our pain and suffering. If you can be patient, there is an entire chapter dedicated to victimhood. For now, be a victor and not a victim.

With this in mind, let me exhort you to stand firm in your beliefs. Don't let your beliefs get trampled underfoot by anyone. I'm not advocating a sense of entitlement by any stretch of the imagination. Wisdom would expect nothing less of us.

Points to Ponder

1. *If you haven't already done so, write down some of the more grievous events in your life.*

2. *What were some of the lessons gleaned from these events? Write these down as well.*

3. *To whom can you impart these lessons? If you have a family, that is a great place to start.*

4. *Don't be afraid to be a mentor to a younger colleague or friend.*

Chapter 12
ACCEPTING

I will not be judgmental of others, not accept
judgments, not put judgments on myself

The time was about two thousand years ago. An up-and-coming rabbi was in the Jewish temple courts, teaching in front of a large crowd when the religious elite of the day, the pharisees, marched up to him with a woman in tow. Being resentful of the young rabbi and wanting to trap him in the Law of Moses, they brought this woman who was "caught in the act of adultery." They demanded an answer to their question of what the rabbi, Jesus, thought should be done, as the law was specific in punishment: that the offending party be stoned (to death, with rocks, not drugs). Jesus' response was very telling, much of which was by what was NOT said. Jesus didn't try and reason with them by His interpretation of the law, nor did He try and philosophize with them. They did seem to have Him over a barrel, as there were "two or three witnesses" bearing testimony. As you may or may not recall, every issue was determined on the basis of two or three witnesses.

The point of the story is simply to see how the woman was handled, or how she was judged. When we begin to politicize and weaponize our laws and traditions, we inevitably become judgmental. We tend to hold ourselves and our standards in higher regard than the people we are in relationship with. A classic example is the dinner table. There are certain things that simply do not happen when we are eating or when we are at the table. This is especially true with young kids. The table is treated better than the kids we are trying to train. The table, that inanimate object, has become a sacred thing, holy ground, and far more valuable than the spirits and souls of any kid who dares do something other than behave as though in the presence of royalty.

When we do this, inevitably, it will be done to us. We will be held to the same standards we hold others to. Such is the nature of being judgmental.

We have witnessed this politicization and weaponization in our culture. This has become manifest in North American society. One of the reasons for this can be blamed on what I call our *soundbite society,* or our *sitcom society.* What do I mean by this? Simply, we want to hear ourselves talk, be it verbally or in print. The things that we say are generally brief, pithy one-liners, often meant to put people in their place, not unlike what we see in modern-day sitcoms. If someone does not adhere to your viewpoint, there is no longer room for critical dialogue or discussion. There is no room to change one's mind or position. This, of course, is grossly oversimplified.

This leads to an inner aspect of judging and being judgmental, and that is **pride.** Since pride is often "bigger than a mouthful," it is often hard to swallow. So hard, in fact, that we won't even try. That would take some humility. We find it extremely difficult to say, "I was wrong; you were right." For example, I don't like making statements regarding my opinion anymore. Instead, I will ask questions to encourage dialogue. These questions are intended to get people to think critically about the positions they hold. This seems to take the "judgmentalness" out of the equation, or at least, that is the intention.

One of the difficulties regarding the second part of the subtitle to this section, *Not Accepting Judgments,* is that judgments seem to be attacks against us. These judgments lead us to believe, rightly or wrongly, that we have been misunderstood. This feeling of being misunderstood tends to weigh on us, and we become defensive.

There is a popular meme that says, "Don't take criticism from anyone you would never go to for advice." We can just as easily say not to accept judgments from anyone you wouldn't go to for advice. I liken this to my old analogy of not wearing clothes that don't fit. If we wear clothes that are too big, we look silly. If we wear clothes that are too small, we still look silly. When we accept judgments and criticisms that don't fit, we *feel* silly. Okay, maybe "silly" is the wrong word. We certainly feel violated, even defiled. Certainly misunderstood.

There are those instances, however, when the criticism or judgment fits. What do we do then? Just likes clothes in the closet, we "wear" it. By this, I mean that we seriously, honestly, and critically evaluate what was said, and if it has some truth to it, accept it, make some course corrections in life to deal with the issues, and move on, thanking the person who cared enough to share these issues.

One thing that I developed into an art form, or science, while working as an immigration officer, was the ability to not take things personally. I would get lied to on a daily basis, called all kinds of evil names, and mean epithets were thrown my way constantly. And that was from my fellow officers. Just kidding. We, as officers, were all in the same boat together. What was interesting was how different individuals handled it. Some would lash out in anger, matching emotion for emotion with the person in front of them. Their behavior, whether right or wrong, was very predictable. If someone escalated in emotion or vitriol, so would the officer.

My approach was different. There was no equity with the people, meaning, I had nothing invested in them, and they had nothing invested in me. I had a motto that went, "Respect for others is not earned, it is given." What I meant by that was I was going to respect everyone from the outset; they would have to earn my "disrespect." I would believe everyone was telling me the truth until what they were saying didn't make sense. My point in this whole discussion is to illustrate how *not* to react to the words and emotions levelled against you. And how to respond to the criticisms and judgments that do echo within your spirit.

I began this section with a famous story from antiquity. I am going to bypass the guts of the story and cut to the chase—the chase being how Jesus dealt with the woman. It is interesting to note the fact that Jesus did not reject the woman, did not humiliate her in front of the crowd, but he did offer some words of encouragement, kind of. In a round-about way, he offered redemption. Hear his words: "Neither do I condemn you…" It can be argued that he saved her life, as she was about to receive the punishment that was to be meted out according to the religious law at the time, specifically, death. He then offers some hope: "Go, and sin no more." He let that sinful woman go unpunished. He told her to go, as in away, back to her life. "And sin no more." He offered her the freedom to live a life without the burden of sin.

Shifting gears…

If there is one thing that I have learned over the years, and I've learned many things, it's that in my younger days (the first thirty-seven years), I could have been easily labelled as a "screw up." Actually, that should be all caps: SCREW UP. If I could make a bad decision or judgment call, I would naturally do it. Oftentimes, my bad decisions and judgments came in the form of characterizing people. They say that first impressions are so important. A good first impression certainly is beneficial, if not expeditious, in a relationship. My issue was two-fold: My judgments got me stuck in a cycle of bad decisions, missing out on some great relationships, and I didn't think to take into account how I may have presented myself, of how *I* came across. Okay, maybe more than two-fold. But it certainly fits in the "screw up" category.

When I finally became aware of my judgmental attitude and behavior, I finally realized that my pointing the finger at people resulted in three fingers coming back at me, to coin a cliché. I didn't realize that, as I judged, so was I judged. It took some pretty tough lessons to figure this out, but thankfully, the lessons seemed to take.

We have all been told "don't judge." Although this is good advice, it leaves out much of what was originally said. The saying actually goes "Judge not, lest you be judged. For with what judgment you judge, you will be judged, and with the measure you use, it will be measured back to you." The gist of the quote is "Don't judge if you aren't going to be fair in your judgment." This still allows for some critical thinking, as people will always judge. The purpose of the quote, if I may oversimplify, is to avoid a hypocritical spirit in our dealings with others, to deal with our issues before pointing out the issues in other people's lives.

Having said all of this, it doesn't say "don't judge, period." What it does say, however, is that if we do judge, do it right; make a right judgment. Have your own life in order; don't speak about things that you have no right speaking about. Don't speak about things or issues that you haven't overcome yourself. It's such a lose/lose proposition: The person on the receiving end loses, because they feel cheap and used and usually go home feeling worse than when they arrived; the other one losing in this equation is you. First, the other person loses respect for you and thinks you are a jerk, asking what right you have speaking about anything in their lives, and second, when you get home and look at yourself in the mirror, you realize what a jerk you are and then have to go through the reconciliation process with them *and* reconcile with yourself.

The good news is that there is healing and personal growth taking place in your life. The healing usually takes the form of feedback in your life. By feedback, I am referring to the way people experience you, usually in a character-building way. By this, I mean they provide "information" that we don't necessarily want to hear but need to hear, and they point out things we may not see or be looking for. Unfortunately, most people don't know how to give feedback in a constructive, neutral, and beneficial manner, usually waiting until things get "out of hand" with behavioral issues and any feedback is given out of intense frustration and/or anger. Translation: not well received.

One way I have found that works fairly well, not to be confused with touchy-feely psychobabble, is to observe a pattern of behavior, usually the same behavior at least two or three times, and say with a neutral voice, "(name), I experience you as (blank)." "Blank" should be a non-inflammatory term, or at least as non-inflammatory as possible. So, something like, "Bob, I experience you as being controlling." Of course, you will be required to back up your experience with some basis of fact, or it is just your opinion and that can be argued away and made of no consequence.

When things go on for too long, emotions can, and usually do, get in the way of meaningful feedback. This can set the relationship back years, not to mention the growth and healing of the person concerned. For the benefit of all concerned, check your ego and pride at the door, adopt a spirit of humility, and in as neutral and caring a voice as possible, share your concerns. You may experience your friends or associates flying off the handle in rage at you, but if done properly, they will respect and appreciate you in the long run.

Just a quick anecdote, for good measure: I was in a personal-growth seminar when I went through a "feedback" session. Eighty people could have their way with me, if they so choose. A number of people chose, and I was bombarded with negativity about myself. I learned very quickly to differentiate between those who were making sport of me and those who genuinely wanted to see me change, grow, and develop some character. At that time, a mental picture came to mind: It was like going through my closet during spring cleaning, wearing what fit and tossing what didn't. It's the same with criticism. Reach into your heart of hearts, and you will be able to determine what fits and what doesn't. Take to heart what applies to you and make the necessary changes. The rest is junk, so just toss it. It will only eat away at you and keep you stuck in your stuff.

When it comes to the difficult situations we find ourselves in, and people we find ourselves with, I have found that, if I don't take things personally, life tends to be far less confrontational and stressful. Part of the process of becoming more accepting of others is, once again, borne out of humility. When we can accept differences as differences and not personal attacks, life will be so much easier.

It seems as though, in today's western culture, many have adopted an "us and them" mentality. It has gotten so severe that the protests that start out peacefully usually end in violence. People being offended, or taking offense, at the smallest things is becoming rampant. Okay, back in my younger days, the major issues of today were not so major back then. There were still some very strongly held opinions, but we tended to agree to disagree peacefully back then. Oh, there were still some violent clashes and fights, but we *tended* to be more peaceful.

Accepting everyone, equally.

As I write this, early June of 2020, North America is under siege by what can be easily described as race riots. If everyone got treated equally, we would either have a lot of dead perpetrators or no dead perpetrators who died needlessly, were *everyone treated the same.* My point is that, whether you are a cop, security guard, crosswalk attendant, teacher, sanitation worker, pro athlete, whatever, we as a society need to treat everyone the same all the time. We need to take our jobs seriously, treating everyone with respect. I have said it before, I will say it again, and will likely say it more, if we were to *give* respect and dignity to everyone we come in contact with, rather than making them *earn* it, we would be much farther ahead as a society.

Points to Ponder

1. *What areas, and whom, do you tend to judge the harshest?*

2. *Are these areas or people, whom you judge, areas or people that you yourself struggle with or are like?*

3. *What strategies can you put in place to avoid being judgmental?*

4. *What strategies can you put in place to be more accepting?*

Chapter 13
JOY

I will choose joy, regardless of my circumstances.

James 1:2 in the Bible, we are exhorted to "consider it pure joy when you encounter trials of various kinds." I know what you are thinking, *Who let this lunatic in?* At least, that's what I initially thought. I mean, trials suck. We could all do with fewer trials in our lives. What possible good can come from the crap that we experience? And if we do experience pure joy in our trials, are we as moronic as we are accusing the originator of this saying to be?

Well, the saying doesn't end there: "…knowing that the testing of your faith produces patience. But let patience have its perfect work, that you may be perfect and complete, lacking nothing." Wow! Who knew? To think that the testing of our faith could have such positive benefits. And it all starts with joy. But what is joy?

To begin, joy is not happiness. I submit to you that happiness is an emotion, whereas joy is a state of being. Joy can be defined as "cheerfulness that is calm delight." So often in life, sorrow prepares us for, and enlarges the capacity for, joy. For example, the deeper the hardship or sorrow, the deeper the joy. Happiness comes as a result of a positive experience. We've all heard the phrase "that makes me happy." It would seem that the event itself has a positive effect on us, resulting in happiness. So, what causes joy?

It is my contention that joy is rooted in peace. It is grounds for joy when we come into harmony with the world around us, indeed, living in harmony with ourselves. Being in right relationships is no easy task, but it is doable, if we work at it. By work at it, I mean that we need to do work on ourselves, to change our way of thinking, to even change much of what we have believed about ourselves. One of the main issues that we must reconcile is this: Do we allow our circumstances, or past events, or even people, to control our state of being? Although I will be addressing this in much greater detail in the chapter on "Victimhood," allow me to at least introduce the topic. A victim, simply put, is one who relinquishes control of their behavior, even their state of mind and state of being, to circumstances, events, or people. Victims often become different people when presented with these "issues." When we become aware of our victimhood, and take the requisite steps to eradicate it from our lives, an abiding sense of peace and joy takes over. This should be the goal of each and every one of us.

What I am about to say next could well fall into the category of "flogging a dead horse," but I wouldn't be flogging it if it weren't important. What I am saying here is this: "Don't let yourselves be conformed to the pattern of this world." (Romans 12:2) The worldly pattern, in this case, would have us react to our situations, rather than respond in a positive manner. Those two words are very interesting in their usage, medically speaking: react being negative and respond being positive. How often have you heard, "He's had a reaction to the treatment" as being negative, or "He's responded well to the treatment" as being positive? Anyway, my point is this: negative experiences in today's culture require negative reactions. People must pay for their negative behavior towards us. Inevitably, this leads to more conflict.

The response we should be considering is one of conciliation, forgiveness, and understanding. There are times when people need to be called on their stuff, but they need to be called in a "righteous" manner. If we can change our attitudes and perspectives to include a joyful response to the various trials we encounter, what a different place our world would be.

Another aspect of joy, in the initial quote, is faith. When our faith is tested, and we consider it pure joy, our patience is perfected. It is our faith in God that gives us joy, but not only joy, but hope as well. As you can see, so many attributes of our beliefs are intertwined: love, joy, peace, patience. You take one away, and the rest are affected.

The bottom line is that joy is a life choice. It is like wearing glasses. If the prescription is wrong, everything is blurry. When the prescription is correct, everything comes into focus and becomes clear. Without joy, we seem to be looking through the wrong set of lenses. With joy, we experience the clarity of the life of joy that is available to each of us. Of course, there is more to the whole life experience than joy, but joy is a critical element. My advice? Change your perspective on life. Don't view the antagonistic things in your life as detrimental experiences but rather as beneficial, meant to develop character and peace and patience. It is then that you can begin to consider things with joy.

Anecdote time. My wife and I were going through life woefully aware of a certain absence in our lives. Actually, more my wife than me. I was stuck in addiction and only cared about one thing—actually, two things, and one of them was me. Anyway, to make a very long and sordid story short, my son and his girlfriend got pregnant. Remember the story? Our first grandson was born. Here is the rest of the story:

So, what happened? Well, my wife strongly believes in the power of prayer. She has a strong, unwavering faith and belief in God, through His son Jesus. She had been praying for us for years, six and a half years to be precise. And not only her; she told all her friends the situation and had them praying. Which was fine, but then all her friends new my sordid story. Then, when the girlfriend got pregnant, she began praying in earnest for the child. She prayed specifically that the child would be healthy, not addicted to drugs, and would serve to bring everyone out of addiction. In other words, a miracle baby.

Let's take a moment for a reality check. To pray for a healthy baby was one thing, but for one to be not addicted to drugs, despite having been conceived in addiction and formed in a drug-induced womb is really pushing the limits of reality. But faith isn't bound by reality. Of course, her faith didn't end there. She prayed the child wouldn't suffer any withdrawal symptoms as well. Then she had the unmitigated gall to pray that the baby would serve to bring everyone concerned out of addiction. Come on, seriously? A child would lead us? Novel concept. What is it about God that He seems to favor and bless the audacity of complete, unmitigated faith, when they ask not one, not two, but four or five impossible prayers that definitely defy logic, if not medical science?

In keeping with our topic of joy, and I am in no way an objective source here, that little guy is such a bundle of joy. He is everything we could have hoped for and more. The joy he has brought to this family is immeasurable.

He certainly makes it easy to choose joy, despite the fact that I am a blubbering mess sitting in the local Starbucks as I write this. But it's okay; people are skillfully avoiding me and the puddle I'm now sitting in. And yes, there is joy in being shunned.

In closing, when you get to this point of choosing joy despite your circumstances, life begins to take on a totally different meaning. Instead of living under a constant rain cloud of depression and self-pity, joy brings out the sun, making clear what we see—often things we were blinded to in the past. Clear skies seem to follow those with joy, and those who come in contact with these joyous people also experience the beauty of their lives. Joy can be so contagious. Don't be shy about it; let it out. And don't, under any circumstance, let anyone take this joy away from you. There will be those who will take offense at your sense of joy and will seek to take it away from you. These ones live and even take pride in living in darkness, and they are, understandably, lonely. Misery needs and looks for company. Instead of joining in their misery, choose joy. You have it within you, it's just one simple decision away. God's joy unspeakable is waiting to fill us, if we are willing. Be willing.

Points to Ponder

1. *What is the source of the most joy in your life?*

2. *How do you get more of it?*

3. *What is your joy killer?*

4. *How do you "kill" the joy killer, so it is not present in your life?*

Chapter 14
LOVE

I will be a giver of love just as I am loved

The power of love. Sounds like a Huey Lewis song from *Back to the Future*. Now, I left out a very important word, however. The word "practice." What does it mean to practice the power of love? Let me break it down into some bite-sized morsels.

First, to practice. By its very nature, the word implies effort on our part. We've all heard the phrase "practice makes perfect." Those of us who have been involved in elite sports have taken this one step further. "Perfect practice makes perfect." Big difference. When we practice something imperfectly, then we end up performing the action imperfectly. The way we practice becomes the way we play, following the sport analogy. That is why we are exhorted to practice perfectly. It takes discipline and hard work. I remember my high-school football coach making us do the same drills again and again and again. It would drive me crazy (which for me was a short trip), doing these same drills and movements ad nauseam until we got it perfect. Absolutely hated it, until we became division champions. After attending school and playing in Texas, I returned home and became an assistant coach under the same coach I had come to love to hate, to love. Oddly enough, I embraced the concept of "practicing perfect." Needless to say, it paid off with a provincial/state championship. The first ever won by a team outside of Vancouver.

I say all of this to point out that it worked so well, I promptly quit doing it in my life and suffered the consequences of my laziness. In many ways, I let myself be conformed to the pattern of this world and ended up paying the piper. I kept my head above water for years, living an undisciplined life occupationally and spiritually. Then it all came crashing down in a pile of homelessness, marital separation, poverty, and addiction.

My life was destined for institutionalization, jail, or death. It wasn't until the love of God descended from heaven and transcended my life that His love got me back on track; he started speaking to me again, giving me dreams and visions. More importantly, His love got me back on track spiritually, practicing perfectly the grace and love of God. So, what does that look like?

Love in its purist form is a wonderful, many splendored thing. It has an open and accepting way about it. For example, before my homeless, drug-addicted phase, I was far more critical of others than was healthy for anyone. The term "being judgmental" would certainly fit. Going through a number of years bouncing off the proverbial bottom, I have become far more understanding, less critical, and far slower to jump to conclusions, which inevitably led to a constant state of judgmentalism.

Let's take my views on homelessness for a moment. Where prior to my fall from normalcy I would be openly critical, to my inner circle at least, regarding their plight and station in life, suffice to say that things began to take a radical shift after I got to know them through my situation.

I was watching an episode of *Mysteries at the Museum* recently. It featured a story about a tunnel that was dug underneath the wall in Berlin. It was used to move refugees out of East Berlin and into freedom in the West. The story was about a young German engineering student and his girlfriend who were separated when the wall went up. Distraught, but undaunted, the young engineering student sought the help of fellow students, and they worked up a plan to tunnel underneath the wall and provide a means of getting the love of his life out of her newfound communist utopia and into the evil capitalistic system of the West. They completed digging, and he made a phone call to set up the move west. Unfortunately, he didn't plan on the East German spy organization, the Stasi, also listening to the call.

With plans made, and dates and times set, the girl set out for the journey. However, she wasn't met with the loving embrace from her boyfriend on the other side. In fact, she didn't even make it to the other side as she was intercepted by the secret police, arrested, and sentenced to sixteen months.

Once again, distraught, but undaunted by this turn of events, the boyfriend, Joachim Neumann, found another suitable location, got his team together, and began digging. The suitable location on the East Berlin side was an abandoned bakery. They completed their digging in 1964. They got wise to the Stasi and utilized code words this time, specifically, "Tokyo" as a tribute to the 1964 Tokyo Olympics.

To make a long story short, Neumann and his girlfriend, Christa Gruhle, were reunited, got married, and lived happily ever after.

But wait, there's more! After his adventures foiling the communists and their socialist utopia, Neumann went on to complete his studies as a civil engineer, specializing in the construction of tunnels. One of the more famous tunnels he worked on was the Chunnel, connecting Paris to London underneath the English Channel.

Such is the power of love. There is no power on earth stronger than the power of love. Love makes us do crazy, unthinkable things, like dig a tunnel under a wall that was constructed to subjugate the citizenry and guarded by a police force who became known for their terror and spying tactics, which they employed to keep their iron boots on the necks of their people. Which leads me to my next point:

It has been said that perfect love casts out fear. That was certainly the case with Neumann. It has also been said that "love covers a multitude of sins." What do these two phrases mean, exactly? In the case with Neumann, it was fairly obvious that the love for his girlfriend, the desire to be reunited with her, trumped everything else, including his own personal safety and well-being. You see, love looks beyond ourselves and sees the object of our love. As a man, I can honestly say there are people I would die for. My wife, my son, my daughter, my four grandsons. There is my sisters' family and my wife's sisters and family. My point is that there are people I am connected to and who I would do anything to protect. This isn't anything heroic; it's simply love. Men and women go to war to fight for their country, for an ideal, a way of life. For some, it is nothing more than a duty, but for others it is a love of country, a love of freedom. Whatever it is, it goes beyond us; it is outward looking. But what causes love to cast out fear? Well, so often it is the fear of rejection that holds us back. Love, by its very nature, is accepting, thereby assuaging any fears of rejection. There is also the fear of failure. With love present, when we fall and fail, love will pick us back up, dust us off, and bring us back into the fold. It is the accepting nature of love.

The second phrase is quite interesting. If we take the religious component out of the equation, the "sins," and replace it with "issues," or "problems," we can see that love trumps all. Love is understanding; it is patient and kind. There are no scorecards of all our wrongs with love. On the one hand, love has an incredible memory; it remembers the good, the virtuous, the reasons that love is present. On the other hand, it is exceptionally forgetful, not remembering wrongs and slights.

Love doesn't come easy; it takes work. Sometimes this work can be very toilsome and tedious. As we work on our relationships and on our love in those relationships, what began as hard and tedious becomes like nothing. In fact, as *we* work on *our* relationships, much of the toil and tedium gets left behind. Love changes behavior. Love changes habits.

With respect to love changing lives, I would be remiss in not mentioning the persevering nature of love. Love is overcoming. True love does not take no for an answer. Love may need to overcome some very big hurdles, some very dire hurdles, but they are hurdles that can be overcome, nevertheless. These hurdles may take some creativity to overcome, but love is worth it. When there is love, there is usually peace accompanying it.

Of course, no discourse on love would be complete if the concept of humility wasn't mentioned. First, there is no room in a love relationship for pride and boasting. A sure destroyer of a relationship is the presence of arrogance. Arrogance is ugly; love is beautiful. When the purpose of the relationship is relating to the other person, then the best interests of the other person become paramount. There is no room for selfishness. We need to make room in our lives for the needs and wants of the other person. This means less of us and more of them. We become givers rather than takers. Life is no longer all about "me;" it becomes about you and us. It is important for us to realize what is being said here. When I say it is not only about me, what I am saying is that love is about *me **and** you,* not necessarily in that order.

It has been often said that the opposite of love is not hate but indifference. I would suggest that the opposite of love is selfishness. Why? Simply because love is "other" focused and not self-focused. When we are more concerned with ourselves, we are less likely to be concerned as much as we should be about our loved ones. Relationships often break down because one of the partners' needs aren't being met. This is a departure from the question asked in a healthy relationship: "How can I meet your needs?" Love gives in a relationship; selfishness takes. A loving relationship is *not* "give and take" but rather give and *receive*. Semantics, maybe, but fairly accurate, nevertheless.

If we remember our wedding vows—if you are married—you will remember it being said that the two have become one. Love is a unifying force. Love honors the other person. It becomes far less self-seeking and far more *us*-seeking. That means no more secrets, no more lies. There is only room for truth in a loving relationship.

If there is one thing our world needs much more of, it is love. In a time when division, disunity, self-righteousness, and self-centeredness are becoming the norm; to see true love in action becomes refreshing like a cool breeze on a hot summer's day. If you do anything today, try and show a little love, especially to someone who is unlovely, or in a volatile situation. Watch the difference love makes.

Points to Ponder

1. *Who are the people, places, or things that you give your love to?*

2. *How can you deepen your love for someone?*

3. *What are some areas in your life that are keeping you from a deeper love relationship?*

4. *Are there any areas in your life where forgiveness needs to be extended or asked for?*

Chapter 15
VULNERABILITY

I will be vulnerable, opening myself
up for others to see inside.

How does one talk about love and not mention vulnerability? It is like describing daylight and not mentioning the sun. Consider this the "confessions of a 'stoic' man, a rock, a steel trap not letting anyone or anything in or out."

I grew up with the adage, "Laugh and the world laughs with you; cry and you cry alone." It taught me that crying was bad, and laughing was good. So, when the need for tears came, I stifled the urge to shed them. I put on a "happy face" and moved on with life. Of course, when personal pain came, or great disappointment came, I would go home, crash on my bed, and cry alone. It's what I learned.

I became very unaware of my feelings, and by extension, the feelings of others. Tears became a sign of weakness to me and for me. When something emotional happened, I stuffed it down, stifled it, and moved on. Not exactly a healthy recipe for an abundant spiritual life. Of course, today, in 2021, I have become a weepy, teary-eyed man, who sheds tears at the slightest good news or bad news.

Unfortunately, I was not alone in this warped, twisted dysfunction. The western world seems to have spawned a generation of "steel trap" people, both men and women. Relationships become warped and twisted with this mindset of not letting anyone in, not showing weakness of any sort. In our "soundbite" society, there is no room for vulnerability. Having said that, the advent of the discussion on mental health has formed pockets of people who are opening up about their struggles. My only concern about this is the potential for trolls to upset the mental-health apple cart. People can be very unforgiving, stuck in their own dysfunction and uneducated disbelief, and thereby, very mean in how they present their "strength."

By now, I would hope that you can see, gentle reader, that I have over-come my need to hide behind a façade of strength and toughness, and being generally closed off to the world around me. I am no longer afraid to share my (myriad and epic) weaknesses, plural. I have found it extremely cathartic (cleansing, healing) to live and express my weakness. A quick look at the twelve steps shows that step one is a confession of weakness. I would hazard to say that my greatest "strength" is my abject weakness. I can honestly say two things: The first is that I did not overcome my addiction, get clean, and start living responsibly because I was strong. In fact, here in the Starbucks where I am writing this, I laughed out loud in reading that last sentence. In fact, this leads me to the second point, and for the most part, that is step three in the twelve steps. I decided to turn my will and my life over to the care of God, as I understand him.

Left to my own devices, I would be in jail, an institution, or dead, to use the AA/NA/CA mantra. I had to tear down the solid and thick walls of strength and independence, and replace them with walls of weakness, vulner-ability, and openness. That means my walls had to include some windows, some glass, some doors, and even some screen doors. These are included to be able to see out, to get out, and just as important, to allow people to see in and even come into my life. To continue the metaphor, there are locks on the doors and windows, and I still have control over who gets in and who doesn't. It only seems prudent to live this way. It seems to be working okay, so I think I will continue to live this way, being open to adapting, should the need arise.

A quick aside here, when speaking of walls. Walls, in my humble opinion, have been vilified by many in pop culture. Tear down your walls, we are told. Although it may sound good, walls serve a very important purpose in a building structure. They hold everything together; they provide protection from the elements, warmth, somewhere to put your roof, and something to anchor the second floor of your building to. Good walls are placed on a solid foundation; in western civilization, that foundation is made of concrete. It shouldn't be going anywhere. My point in this whole discussion is to illustrate that walls can be a good thing when used properly, when used for the reason they are put there in the first place. When we as people construct walls around our persons, the walls should be used for protection and shelter from the onslaught of attacks that come our way from friends and enemies alike. Let in people who are safe, who you want to visit with and share your life story with. If people are trying to hurt you, don't let them in. The key is to use the walls judiciously, for your benefit and for the benefit of those around you. After all, people want to know the real you, baggage and everything. Let them in. Back to being vulnerable.

If our close relationships are to survive, or even thrive, then the art of being vulnerable needs to be practiced. How many relationships have been dashed on the rocks of aloofness, being stoic, closing oneself off to the other, and not accepting the other's feelings? The whole concept of emotional connections needs to be explored and studied. It is these emotional relationships with one another that provide the bond and the mortar that many relationships are lacking but are so desperately needing.

Vulnerability is something that we should all embrace. Unfortunately, it seems to be shunned by many, mainly out of fear. Fear, it seems, would be the enemy of vulnerability. We act out of fear. Our behavior is often dictated out of fear. We close up and shut down out of fear. We lash out because of fear. What are we afraid of? If I may oversimplify, often it is the fear of exposure, the fear of loss and rejection. We fear that we will lose our friendships if people get to see inside. If they see us for who we *really* are, they won't like us.

It has been said that "what we fear, we create." For our purposes here, if we fear losing friends because they won't like us once they get to know us, and we shut ourselves down and don't let them in, guess what? Before long, we will need to look for new friends, because these ones will get tired of trying to get to know us.

It seems so counterintuitive to open up and let people in. Why would we subject ourselves to the possibility of pain and rejection? The crazy thing is, when we become vulnerable and let people in, so often, they stick around after they enter. To continue with the metaphor, when they come in, they will find a comfy chair and settle in, taking in the décor, which is your inner life, your fears, your dreams … the things that give you healthy pride.

On a personal note, since I have opened up about my failures, my homeless/addiction issues, the temporary estrangement from my wife, and my subsequent victories in life, I have found that, instead of being shunned and ostracized, I have been accepted, and brought back into the fold of my immediate and extended family and friends. Talk about a reversal in life, a total change in direction and mindset. Where I would put on different masks to keep people at bay, they would stay at bay. In fact, the bay seemed to get bigger and bigger, meaning that they got further and further away from me, both physically and emotionally. When the masks came off, people seemed to get closer, opening themselves up to me, and the bonds seemed to get stronger. When I no longer feared losing friends because they saw the real me, I opened up, bared my soul, and gained new respect from my family and friends. Such is the power and beauty of vulnerability.

Honesty with oneself is absolutely necessary when becoming vulnerable; indeed, it is the necessary first step. Of course, we also have to be honest with others when being vulnerable. Anything other is simple manipulation in its worst and most vile form.

Points to Ponder

1. *What is keeping you from being vulnerable? Fear or pride or simply being unaware of the need to be vulnerable?*

2. *What are some first steps in your walk of vulnerability?*

3. *Who are some of the important people in your life you should be vulnerable with?*

Chapter 16
PATIENCE

I will be patient with myself and with others.

Aahhh, patience. It's something that I want, and I want it NOW. Riiight. Talk about counterculture. Having to wait for something in our instant, fast-food, microwavable, 4G, soon to be 5G, culture? Please tell me you are kidding. And to have to work on it to actually get it???? Come on, seriously?

Such are the vagaries of dealing in and with the spiritual life. Nothing comes easy; it takes work. Many of the spiritual disciplines that are mentioned in this book are in conflict with our human nature, our learned behavior and thought patterns. One of the hardest of the spiritual disciplines to master is, of course, patience. And patience, ironically, takes time.

Very quickly, an old English word for patience was, "longsuffering" and another way of looking at this is with the word, "forbearance." Longsuffering. Isn't that an apt way of looking at patience? Suffering in wait for a long time. It definitely builds character. But is that what patience is, exactly? Let's take a closer look, shall we?

Before we look at patience, let's look at some issues that hinder the growth and development of this important spiritual discipline.

First, let's deal with personal expectations, or what we expect from ourselves. So often, we place seriously unrealistic expectations on ourselves. For some reason, we have been led to believe that we are supposed to be super humans, and as such, believe we should be far more accomplished than we are. There is little room for failure or mistakes of any kind. Anything less than perfection is unacceptable. You may recall that earlier I mentioned practicing perfect. Inevitably, despite our perfect practicing, we will make mistakes in real-time competition. Fact of life. So, what's the point? Not only does that minimize our mistakes, but it also mitigates them. The truly great competitors fully understand this and are completely aware that they will screw up somehow. This doesn't mean that they are happy when it happens. It all comes back to the "response/react" concept also mentioned earlier. The great ones adapt and adjust and perform accordingly. One thing that separates the good from the great is how patiently they ply their craft. They make mistakes, accept them, control themselves in spite of them, and move on to accomplish what they set out to do. Many times, they prepare for the inevitable occurrence of mistakes, all the while waiting patiently for their opponent to make a mistake. Further to this, in a sports-psychology way, they use the mistake to propel them to greatness, often on the next play, or at least, later in the match. This patient mindset is what makes them great.

The great American philosopher Lawrence (Yogi) Berra, former catcher for the Yankees, commented one day that, "Ninety percent of the game is half mental." Such profundity just doesn't exist anymore (he said, tongue firmly planted in cheek). His point, of course, was that in sports, the "mental game" was like the "red-headed step-child" of the family. Not much thought was given to it, or at least back in Yogi's day. But I digress. My point is, like all spiritual disciplines, patience takes discipline, forethought, and of course, patience. Please note, I have nothing against red-headed step-children, simply a reference to a past way of thinking, when red-headed orphans were some of the least likely to be adopted.

A quick word on how the mental game should work: When I was coaching in college, I taught my team about what I called, "The Competitive Process." This process consisted of three very specific, yet totally different items. Every play had them in a specific order. Mastering them was no easy thing. The first was "preparation." Volleyball, played at an elite level, is a fast sport; you need to be quick on your feet, able to think even quicker. The bulk of the preparation process took place between serves, when there was actually time to regroup, both as a team and individually. Where things got really interesting was when a rally continued back and forth over the net a few times. I called these the "championship" rallies for the simple fact that only the great players could think fast, think ahead, anticipate, adjust, and adapt to what the other team was doing. This was all part of the greater preparation that a team went through, so that during the game, the players didn't have to stop and think.

The second part of the competitive process was "behavior," or the act of performing the proper moves and plays. The players were only responsible for the moves and plays that they, and they alone, could perform, the plays and moves that were in their control. They weren't responsible for anyone else's behavior other than their own. If they did something that totally "crapped the bed," they were to own it, take responsibility for it, and leave it in the past. They can't change what they have done, only change what they are about to do. And even that is contingent on a number of factors. In broad strokes, the proper adjustments can be made, the first of which starts between the ears with acceptance of one's actions.

Which leads to our third process in the competitive process: response. I have alluded to it in the behavior process, but it is clearly a distinct process that continues on well past each play. This is essential to master when in competition. The proper response to a given situation can be the difference in bringing a team out of the pit or keeping them in the pit and going deeper. It is interesting to watch a match unfold. Just watch the shoulders of the athletes. If they do well, their shoulders are back and up, proud of their accomplishments. If their performance is somewhat less than stellar, the shoulders will often droop forward. You have to be quick and know what to look for, but it happens, especially as the match goes on.

So how does all that relate to patience? Well, the great athletes are well aware of what they are capable of. If they screw up, they are patient with themselves, cutting themselves some slack, knowing that screw up won't be happening again any time soon. But patience extends even further. If they get beaten on a certain play, they acknowledge it, accept it, and adjust so it doesn't happen again. In fact, what I used to do in sports, when beaten on a play, was actually feign getting beaten again the same way. What I was doing was adjusting my game to get the upper hand. I was very patient with this, waiting until the opportune time to "spring my trap." But spring it I would, much to the chagrin of my opponent.

The key here is knowing who you are and what you are capable of. When you know yourself that well, patience can truly be a virtue, to be used to your advantage. So, my question is this: Why is this so much easier in sports than in real life? Well, sports are a microcosm of life, and if sports are the micro, then everyday life is the macro. What I mean is, unless you're competing at the professional level and on TV, the average match will only last a couple of hours, at best. Life, on the other hand, is considerably longer in duration. Where plays happen "bang-bang" one right after another, life takes a little longer to unfold. The principles apply in life every bit as much as in a sports match. We need to prepare, to practice, and to study our competition. Same as in life. We then have to go about our duties, or behavior, performing our "moves" in life. Then comes the appropriate response, regardless of the outcome. Where patience comes in is during the long periods of time between events in our lives. I call this the "attitude killing" time. When we are left alone with our thoughts, our failings, regrets, and misgivings, and we are not comfortable with who we are, the door for disaster is left wide open. Be patient with yourself; life is filled with grief and failing. It's how you pick yourself up after these setbacks that will determine your destiny in life.

Back to personal expectations. It is safe to say that one's level of disappointment is proportionate to their level of expectation. The higher the expectation, the higher the level of disappointment when failure comes knocking, or when the expectation is not met. If we don't have patience with ourselves, this disappointment will eat us alive. In closing, there is a huge difference between unreasonable expectations and reasonable, achievable goals. Take the time to do an inventory between the two, but please, be reasonable. If you want to give yourself something for Christmas, give yourself a break, especially when it comes to yourself and any unreal expectations that you may have set for yourself.

One thing that I should mention here is this: You don't have to be an island unto yourself. In fact, allow me to rephrase this: *Don't be an island unto yourself.* In the context of our discussion on setting realistic goals and having realistic expectations, allow others to be involved as a sounding board in order to give you healthy feedback. These should be people you trust and respect, who will be honest with you, and who will hold you accountable.

Next, let's think about others. Sometimes, having patience with others is much easier than having patience with ourselves. Any guesses as to why? Perhaps it's because we have far fewer expectations on others than we do on ourselves. My real question is this: Why do we put so much pressure on the ones we love and have such high expectations of them? It's not like they don't have enough pressure from everyone and everywhere else to contend with. Perhaps if we extended some grace and compassion towards them, some of that will manifest in patience for them.

After having patience for others, our next task is to control our tongue. "How does this relate to patience?" you ask. Well, anytime we exhibit self-control, we also exhibit a modicum of patience. If we actually think before we speak, we exhibit patience. When we come to the point in our lives where we don't have to hear the sound of our own voices, we have taken a major step in our spiritual journey. I know I have mentioned this previously, but it bears repeating here. If we can take the time to formulate our thoughts, control our emotions, and maintain a certain neutrality, we begin to demonstrate a level of maturity that we can be proud of. Of course, there may be times when neutrality may seem counterproductive and some passion for what is spoken would be in order. That's fine. There are times that controlled passion is required. This takes some discernment.

A very important concept to remember is the cliché: Actions speak louder than words. True enough, for both good and bad. A well-thought-out response, a well-planned action, realizing that sometimes no action is what is called for, all these can be life-changing events. The opposite is also true. Being reactionary can bring devastation and destruction. Flying off the handle does no one any good. And not even flying off the handle but simply not thinking things through before speaking or acting can be equally destructive. This is where patience comes in, big time.

Just as love can cover a multitude of sins, so can patience, but in a different way. By not reacting to a situation and simply letting it pass, you are, in essence, showing the other person that you respect them enough to treat them with grace and compassion. By giving a measured response to a given situation/episode, you speak volumes to the person concerned that you value their feelings and emotional health. The upside to this can be staggering. The person will be shocked by your response of not blowing up, or stating the obvious, or replying sarcastically, thereby demeaning them. Think about this: Ask yourself how you would like to be treated and treat others accordingly. Simple "golden rule" stuff. Amazing how this simple little "rule" will affect your life.

Which brings us to the question of control. Usually, a question we try to avoid, especially for the Alpha/type-A people among us. Actually, there are probably not many of those reading this, as they probably have their lives in control and everyone around them in control, as well. Just kidding. But not.

If we are honest, we will admit this is a disturbing trait that we often employ, much to the chagrin of others, and even our own chagrin. I will be addressing this at length in the session on "victimhood," but suffice to say that, more often than not, we are controlled by our situations at least as much as we control them. In this case, being in control is a good thing. It's the type of control that is really quite beneficial, especially when used with discernment. It becomes a matter of how much control do you want to exhibit in a certain situation. What I mean is that there are situations that may warrant a certain emotional response—a controlled emotional response, but emotional, nonetheless. Again, more on this later.

Then comes the issue of what to do when we lose control, or let a situation dictate our behavior. Well, we can wallow in our failure, chalking circumstances up to a character flaw, or we can pick ourselves up, dust ourselves off, and look at this a profound learning experience. The choice is ours and ours alone. Choose the latter.

One more aspect of having patience. This takes on the form of advice. When conflict, pain, missed expectations, et cetera, hit us, one "response" I have taken or maintained is that I don't take it personally. Generally speaking, it wasn't intended personally. When I was an immigration officer, I would be lied to, insulted, my genetics and family history questioned, and even challenged physically in the form of violent rebellion. The one thing I *didn't* do was take it personally. Why would I? They didn't even know me. They were acting out of their own hurt and pain. I happened to be the one in front of them at the time. When younger officers would get exercised over some of the issues mentioned above, I would give them the same advice I tried to live by: Don't take it personally. Have patience. Adopting this attitude worked wonders in de-escalating situations that were starting to get out of hand. I would simply sit there and let them vent, waiting patiently for them to "gas out." Of course, if they were loud, and their venting was profanity laced, I would firmly, yet calmly, intervene. I found that if I waited patiently for them to blow off some of the pressure that had built up, things would settle down and we could carry on.

When we realize that life isn't a destination but a journey, we will be that much further ahead on the path of life. These obstacles in life are simply speed bumps designed to slow us down, and make us regroup, smell the coffee, drink the coffee, and patiently, move on.

Points to Ponder

1. *What areas of your life could use more patience?*

2. *With whom could you be more patient?*

3. *Are your expectations of yourself and others reasonable?*

4. *What changes can you make in your expectations and behaviors to become more patient?*

5. *How much time do you spend preparing yourself to become more patient?*

Chapter 17
KILLING THE VICTIM, BEFORE THE VICTIM KILLS YOU

I will be in control of my life, not abdicating control
to anyone, any past event, or past circumstance.

As a victor, I am responsible for my thoughts and actions. I will blame no one, no event or circumstance, nothing, for my state in life, cognitively or behaviorally.

Years ago, I came in contact with a book titled, *Killing the Victim Before the Victim Kills You.* A compelling title, but little else. Not to be rude, but they could have done so much more. Indeed, the few words that I am going to spend here will not do the subject justice. My apologies in advance. I will attempt to hit the high points of the subject to give you enough to change your attitudes and outlook on life.

So, how to define "victim"? Here is my humble attempt: A victim is someone who relinquishes control of their lives to some person, event, or circumstance, blaming said person, event, or circumstance, and not taking responsibility for their words, actions, or behaviors. I liken it to being handcuffed, emotionally, that is. When we know that we should respond in a certain way, when we want to respond that way, but don't because we are afraid or conditioned not to, then we are handcuffed. Specifically, we are a victim to that event or person. It controls our response by negating it. We become victims, plain and simple.

Unfortunately, victimhood is in our DNA. Looking back to the story of Adam and Eve, we find them in the garden with only one rule to follow: Don't eat from the tree of the knowledge of good and evil. Should have been simple enough. Unfortunately, that wily old serpent had other plans. As the story goes, the serpent came to Eve and said, "Surely you won't die if you eat from the tree." As fate would have it, she succumbed and showed her hubby, Adam, that she, in fact, did not die. So later, when God was wandering through the garden, He couldn't see our two intrepid forebears and called out to them. They replied they were hiding, because they were naked. The inevitable question came out, "Who told you that you were naked?" Adam's response was classic: "It's all her fault, the woman YOU gave me." Of the three around at the time, Adam blamed two and virtually absolved himself of any blame.

He blamed God, who put "that woman" in the garden with him. Some "help-meet" she was. And in true husband fashion, he then turned his blame towards the only other person on earth: his wife, Eve. And we wonder why the world is the way it is. But it's easy to criticize Adam, isn't it? I'm sure we all would have behaved admirably and nobly, with honor, taking full responsibility for our actions. Actually, I'm sure we would have all risen above the temptation and refused the forbidden fruit altogether. Right, and I have some well-irrigated land in south Florida for sale.

Hindsight being 20/20, we can, at least, learn from the mistakes made in the garden, especially as it relates to the topic of victimhood.

To begin with, there was the initial temptation. My point here, is that there are many competing voices for our attention and not all of them are good. I have listed a number of spiritual precepts to live by previously, and we would do well to follow them. Regardless, establish for yourselves a set of precepts/rules that are non-negotiable, concepts that are virtually etched in stone for your lives, and don't ever deviate from them. That way, when the "serpents" of life show up, tempting you to deviate from the path you have set out, the answer is clear: Just say no to the issue and follow the path set before you. This is easier said than done. Remember to give yourself a break, use any misstep as a learning experience, have patience with yourself, and move onward and upward. Before long, you will become accomplished in discerning between the bad voices and good voices, and life will become far more manageable.

It is important at this point to mention the concept of weakness as it relates to victimhood. Weakness, in and of itself, can either be a good thing or a not-so-good thing. For example, as was mentioned previously, when I was coming out of addiction, I embraced my weakness, acknowledged that I was weak, and left things in God's hands. I didn't try to "outmuscle" my weakness, as that approach had failed miserably innumerable times in the past. I simply relinquished the control that weakness had on me to my higher power and let him deal with it. And deal with it he did.

Accompanying, and acknowledging, weakness is humility, or being humble. Where great things can be done with one's weakness, the only thing to be done with one's pride is bringing the person low. Think of it as a "forced humility project." I have found in my life that, when I have been proud (most of my adult life), situations have arisen in my life that I have been less than proud of, real "head-shaking" moments that I have felt humiliated by. Now, I may be a lot of things, but stupid isn't one of them. It took a while, but I realized that "if I did what I always had done, I would get what I always got." My thinking was that I would change my thinking, talking, and behavior. Funny thing was, things started to change in my life with the advent of humility.

Then there is faith. Once again, the presence of faith includes the presence of humility. Faith, in this case, refers to believing in something more than oneself. To have faith in something, we have to look beyond ourselves and to something greater than ourselves. This means denying ourselves and relying on the object of our faith. This is also the birthplace of hope, and as it has been said somewhere, without hope, the people perish.

Unfortunately, there are many competing "voices" vying for our attention. Many of these voices, indeed all of them, are generally negative. Upon closer examination, we see this is where victimhood rears its ugly head. That is, if we heed these voices. Life is a series of choices, the most important ones being very simple: We can believe the imaginary voices that are lying to us or not. Simple. I will speak to this in more detail later.

After the "voices" have been dealt with, there is the fact that we don't live life in a vacuum. We all have some interaction with other people, whether we like it or not. Many of these people simply do not have your best interests in mind. In fact, many are very self-serving in their interactions with you. Patiently take the time to sift through the noise and listen to what is right, beneficial, and true. If you get sucked into their web of deception, acknowledge it, and get forgiveness for it—whether the forgiveness comes from yourself or from someone you've hurt—learn from the event, establish a strategy to avoid, adjust and adapt to the next issue, and move on.

An analogy seems to be in order here. Years ago, I had a closet and dresser full of clothes, including old clothes that no longer fit. They were perfectly good clothes, but I had lost some significant weight. Anyway, the clothes that fit, I kept. The ones that didn't, I gave away or tossed. Point being, in life there are voices and people who say things to us that just don't fit. In this case, don't wear them. Toss them, because they aren't worth trying to pull on. Of course, wear the stuff that "fits," embrace it, take responsibility for it, and own up to it. This is the beginning of being a "victor."

A victor is someone, obviously, who overcomes the obstacles and voices that inundate our lives, and lives overcome in all that he or she does. Little, if anything, stops them. Optimism is a given, and there is no room for cynicism in any of their thoughts or endeavors. This is not a "Pollyanna" mindset by any stretch. These are glass-half-full types of people. They see the good in people and events and don't let these things get them down or slow them down.

Some of my heroes, victors, include David (of David and Goliath fame), Jesus (of course), Winston Churchill, Mother Theresa of Calcutta, George Washington, Abraham Lincoln, my grandfather on my dad's side, and my grandparents on my mother's side.

Aside from Jesus, none of these others would remotely consider themselves perfect. What they did have in common were an overcoming spirit, never-say-die attitude, and a fundamental belief in the human spirit for good. My paternal grandfather made the cut because of his actions in the First World War. There wasn't one act that set him apart, but there is a small story. First, he lied about his age to enlist. Many did during those days. He proved himself capable enough to get a promotion from private to corporal and from corporal to sergeant, which he received at the end of the war. One of the main achievements in his young life was fighting for the Canadian forces at Vimy Ridge, the battle that defined Canada as a young nation. Vimy Ridge was a key strategic stronghold held by the enemy. There had been many battles to take it, and all had ended in defeat. This is all cool stuff, but it is what he said to me in 1968 that I have never forgotten. It was April of that year, and on the first Saturday of the month, the sixth to be precise, we were watching the news and the death of Martin Luther King was being broadcast. He had died on Thursday. It was the first and only time I heard him speak of the war. He said he didn't understand why there was such racial hatred in the United States. I asked him why he said that. He simply told me that many Blacks and Asians had fought with him and "given the full measure of devotion" (my words, quoting Abraham Lincoln) in service for their country. He told me to never judge anyone, not by color, religion, or anything. Fifty years later, I am still in tears when I think of what he said. He died the next year.

A quick story about my mother's family is in order. Back around the turn of the twentieth century, my grandparents on my mother's side were living in Russia. They were a very, very successful family, in fact they were so successful that my grandfather had his own tailor. So? Many people had tailors. But my grandfather employed one full-time on his estate. His job was to clothe not only all the family (a total of twelve, including his wife and children) but the entire staff who were employed with the running of the estate, and their families who were also housed on the estate. They had more horses than most estates had sheep and other cattle. Anyway, suffice to say, they were part of the wealthy elite. Land barons. Whatever. As fate would have it, some loud-mouth named Vladimir Ilyich Lenin was growing in popularity, so much so that he was leading a revolt against the Czar and all that he stood for, along with all those like the Czar, specifically the wealthy landowners. Since my grandparents lived out in the sticks on their estate, it took a while for the actual revolutionary army to get to their neck of the woods.

To make a long story short, the workers on the estate warned my grand-parents of the impending doom that was soon to befall them and urged them to get out of the country. My grandmother took the advice to heart, packed up her things and children, and pleaded with her husband to join her. Being very successful and very stubborn, he just couldn't leave all that behind. So, she took off. Well, a day later, he joined them, and they all fled to Canada. Upon arriving at the border with Latvia, they were stopped, and it was found that they were on a "death list." As they were lined up to be shot, my uncle, who was twelve at the time, blurted out, "The jewels are in the baby's bassinet." As it was a rather large bassinet, there were a lot of jewels present. There were also jewels sown into the clothes of the children. This was to fund their lives in the new world. As their executioners were tied up with their newfound treasure (one they would not be sharing with the collective), my grandparents quietly egressed the building and headed across the border, large family in tow. For the record, the baby mentioned above was my mother, who was under a year old at the time. Anyway, they came to Canada with very little. Now, they could have sat around, depressed with the hand they were dealt, wallowing in the crap associated with losing such a huge estate and vast wealth, or they could suck it up and make the best of a bad situation. So, they bought a farm in Saskatchewan just as the dust bowl showed up. More misfortune. Did they quit? No, they moved to British Columbia where they set up in the small farming community of Chilliwack and then moved to Vancouver, where they bought a house and stayed for seventy years. During that time, they bought land, built houses, logged, worked as longshoreman, married, and spawned a bunch of kids. What they didn't do was live as victims. They didn't live as the refugees they actually were. They weren't looking for any handouts and probably would have been offended if any handouts were offered to them. It couldn't have been easy, not knowing the language, the customs, or traditions, living in a totally foreign land. All they had was each other.

Another attribute of a victor is the fact they take responsibility for their actions and words. They don't shift blame, hoping to get away with something or hoping that someone else will take the fall in their stead. When adversity does hit, they hit back, and with a vengeance. They learn from their mistakes and move on, all the while growing in maturity and spirituality.

They don't relinquish control of their lives to anyone or anything, at least, not for very long. It's their lives, and they live it to the fullest. Freedom isn't a word they use; it's a word they live. They allow nothing to hold them back. Fear is a four letter "f" word to be embraced. What?!? You've got to be kidding?? Actually, I'm as serious as a heart attack on this one. Why? Because fear is an illusion. If perfect love can cast it out, then what power does it have? Further, when it shows up and rears its head, look at it as an opportunity to overcome a serious obstacle. We've heard it said so often that, when fear is present, courage is required to overcome it, or words to that effect. Victims shrink under it; victors crush it under their boot and kick it to the curb. Okay, maybe "embrace" wasn't quite accurate. But you get my point, I hope—shock value, and all that.

Back on task. Another thing victors DO NOT DO is blame. They take responsibility for their words and actions. They have to. After all, no one and nothing, save God Himself, holds any control over them. That being said, who's to blame for their words or actions? Yup, they and they alone are responsible. Anything other would make them victims, and that's something they won't stand for. Once again, all we have to do is look at Adam ("the woman who you gave me...") and see the consequences of victimhood. We are all still paying for it, but we can't just look at Adam and blame him now, can we?

Points to Ponder

1. *Who or what have I given control of my thoughts, emotions, and decision-making capabilities?*

2. *Do I take responsibility for my thoughts and actions or do I blame others or things?*

3. *How has being a victim hindered me from having what I want?*

4. *How has being a victim affected my relationships?*

Chapter 18
ACCOUNTABILITY

I will make myself accountable to others
for my thoughts and actions.

I will find friends whom I trust and not worry about being judged. They will have permission to hold me accountable and keep me honest. I cannot do this alone.

Paul Simon may have been a rock and an island in his classic song, but I am not. Not even close. In fact, when I try and be "rock-like," I fail miserably. The fact is, we weren't put on this rock to be alone. Even Adam was given Eve so he wouldn't be alone. When we are left to our own devices, things go terribly wrong. Why is this? Why do we need others? Don't they just get in the way with their own agendas and selfish behavior? "Ain't no one gonna tell me what to do." I will look at a couple of concepts over the next several paragraphs that should help dispel many of the current misconceptions regarding accountability and support.

To rely on others for support takes humility. That word, again. Think about it: The very word "support" means "to bear the weight of; to hold up", or "to lend assistance to; enable to act." This seems to indicate that I can't do it alone. It means there are burdens in life to bear that are too great for me to carry alone. I know, personally, that one of the hardest things in my life is to ask for help ... with anything. Part of that came from my time going to school in Texas, home of the legendary Texas Rangers (not the baseball team, the law-enforcement officers who made their bones in the Wild West of rough and rowdy Texas). The thought that stayed with me for all those years was a motto ascribed to them: "One riot, one Ranger." Tough, self-reliant, motivated, all worthy qualities … for a job. Of course, much of that crossed over to their personal lives, I'm sure. It's hard to picture some of those guys with a grandson bouncing on their knees as a doting grandpa. But again, I digress.

My point is, in my formative years, I was fairly impressionable (some would say gullible), and as such, I embraced some "interesting" points of view. Tough, macho, egotistical, arrogant, cocky points of view. As fate would have it, I met a young lady who was a spiritual, humble (beautiful) person who didn't necessarily appreciate some of my more dominant personality traits. Go figure. Did I mention she was patient? Long story short, we fell in love, got married, spawned a couple of good kids, and all the while, she was whittling away at my tough outer shell, sometimes overtly and sometimes covertly through a deep and abiding faith in God, through prayer. In many of those years, she was my biggest support, though I didn't always acknowledge or admit it. My mother was the same way. My daughter began following in her mother's footsteps. I guess my real question is this: "What is it about women?" Anyone who still believes that women are the "weaker" sex has their head firmly planted where the sun doesn't shine. As my support, she had to bear the weight of my stupidity on so many occasions (not to mention my 230-240 pounds); as a mother, she had to bear the burdens of an adult child stuck in addiction, followed by a husband who got hooked on pain meds and mostly screwed up his life. Through it all, she never lost her faith: in God, in her child, and in me. If anything, it made her stronger.

So how important is having someone, or many someones, as a support mechanism? One of the most successful fellowships in the world is Alcoholics Anonymous. Note the advised use of the word "fellowship." Many people of like mind, with like adversity (read: alcoholism/addiction) would come together and share their stories, hardships, struggles, successes, and failures, all the while doing so in a judgment-free environment. It was formed *by* alcoholics *for* alcoholics. Now, there are literally hundreds of "Anonymous" groups around: cocaine, narcotics, gambling, sex addicts, parents of all of the above, etc. And why have so many groups popped up? Perhaps because the concept of support works.

It should be noted, in light of the previous chapter, that there is more to AA than just sharing your story. There is the "big book" that takes the practitioner through the twelve steps. This is an integral part of the journey: education, learning, growing, changing. There is also the practice of pairing up with a sponsor. The sponsor is the one who provides much of the personal support. The sponsor provides a non-judgmental ear and offers non-judgmental advice and thoughts for success. All in all, AA, and its derivatives, has proven its worth over the decades.

Anecdote time. Back in the sixties, or seventies, a Harvard study into addiction was done using rats as the subjects. A rat was, obviously, placed in a cage and a major amount of cocaine was placed in its water along with another tube of pure water next to it. Needless to say, the poor little rat consistently went for the cocaine, leading researches to conclude that the substance was the issue and the war on drugs began in earnest. Years later, a similar study was done at Simon Fraser University in Burnaby, BC (Vancouver). Now, not to repeat the previous study, the researches added a few twists. The first was using heroin instead of cocaine, and the second, and in my mind, even more significant alteration, was they put a rat family together instead of a single, lone rat. They also built a "rat park," complete with rat paraphernalia, including a treadmill and other fun rat stuff. Inevitably, the rat chose the pure water over the Heroin-laced water. Time after time, the results came back the same: pure water as opposed to drug laced water.[2] Conclusion: the addition of lifestyle alteration was the catalyst to "clean living" in rats.

Another anecdote is in order, this time with humans. It was found that in many Vietnam servicemen during the war, heroin addiction was fairly widespread. The concern was that when these returning soldiers returned home, there would be serious issues with crime and addiction. The shocking news was that, upon their return, many of the soldiers simply stopped using once they were back in their familiar surroundings, complete with work, family, and extra-curricular activities. A few experienced some withdrawal, discomfort, and unease. But many didn't, quitting cold turkey.

So, my obvious question is, why—for the love of all things sacred—don't our politicians divert the untold billions it costs to incarcerate people who,

---

2   Please note that they did not shun the drug-laced water ALL the time, but they certainly did not get addicted to it.

through addiction, got involved in crime, got busted, and now have ruined their lives, falling deeper and deeper into the dark world of drugs and crime, and provide funding for legislated recovery and support programs? Forgive the rant and run-on sentence.

The next step in the recovery journey, spiritual or otherwise, is accountability. In AA, the affected individual has the support of the group at large but is accountable to the smaller group who he/she is going through the steps with. Further accountability is made through the person's sponsor, the individual who has successfully been through the program, can offer a mature, nonjudgmental ear, and is available on call pretty much 24/7.

Accountability, in itself, has a certain intrinsic, spiritual quality, especially within the AA community. In fact, step five states that we are to "admit … to another human being the exact nature of our wrongs." Of course, this is in addition to ourselves and our higher power. Being able to unburden oneself of the shame and guilt that goes along with one's life to another living person is truly a gift from God. But where does this shame and guilt go? Humanly speaking, it is one thing to confess, or admit, our wrongs, and quite another thing to ask for forgiveness. Receiving forgiveness, true forgiveness, is like receiving a pardon, having your record expunged and made clean. In the Christian world, asking God for forgiveness for all the wrong in your life, and giving it over to Him, is all that and more. In fact, it says that "He removes your sin as far as the east is from the west." It's not only forgiven by God but forgotten as well.

To conclude, when we isolate ourselves, we invite disaster. The concept of moral gravity, that unseen force that drags and keeps you down, is made exponentially worse when we are alone, when we isolate. When we surround ourselves with healthy, clean, trustworthy people who won't judge us, we can expect the same healthy, clean life for ourselves. As a word of caution, please keep your eyes open for loved ones who start isolating themselves and who start hanging around with the wrong people. Don't be afraid to confront, in love, but confront, nevertheless. Let them know you expect more from them and that they are better than the path they are heading down. It can be disappointing, but hang in there; believe the best will happen to your loved one, and always let them know you will be there for them.

Points to Ponder

1. *How and why do you isolate?*

2. *List times in your life when isolation has not ended well for you.*

3. *To whom can you be accountable? Who do you trust?*

4. *List three friends, preferably not of the opposite sex (men with men, women with women) and not immediate family, with whom you can be accountable, with whom you share your life's personal story.*

THOUGHTS AND BEHAVIOUR
I <u>WILL NOT</u> PARTICIPATE IN

This is a little departure from where we have been going thus far. Up until now, I have been talking about how we can dig deeper into our lives and become better people, living with less conflict and generally living in peace with others and with ourselves.

The next few chapters will be more negative in nature, looking at behaviors that keep us down, behaviors that are learned, behaviors that we have adopted in order to cope, in order to get what we want out of life, often borne out of personal trauma. We have adopted these behaviors because we seem to think they actually work for us, that they have made us who we are and there is no point in changing. What we fail to realize is that, unless we are total doormats, allowing people to walk all over us, or that our mission in life is to please everyone, there is a wake of spiritual carnage left behind us wherever we go.

I humbly ask that, as you go through these next chapters, you read these next chapters with an open mind, asking yourself the simple question: "Do I do that?" If the answer is yes, make the necessary adjustments.

Chapter 19
SELF-DEFEATING GAMES

Although the clinical team for this is "Self-defeating Learned Behavior," I will simply be referring to these behaviors as "games." So, what is meant by this anyway? As the title suggests, this learned behavior, which we *all* possess in one way or another, is completely and totally self-defeating. This means that whatever it is that we are doing is leading to an unfruitful and depressing existence. Not to make light of the issue, but if we aim a loaded gun at our foot, we will inevitably hit it. Think of shooting yourself in the foot.

Let me refresh your memory. As mentioned earlier in the book, it all starts at the beginning, with the Human Condition. It begins innocently enough, as small children, even as infants. When we are hungry, we cry; when we have a messy diaper, we cry; when we want attention, we cry. As we get older, we learn that when we cry, we get what we want. The louder we cry, the quicker we get what we want. Unless this behavior is nipped in the bud, the simple cry will turn into a full-on tantrum. The skilled practitioner (read: child) will realize early on where the most effective places to ply their skill are, usually in the most inappropriate places imaginable: usually a busy aisle or checkout counter at the local Walmart, or at the playground in front of all the "good" little kids and their perfect parents, or heaven forbid, in church (pun intended). You get the point.

Of course, parents are somewhat complicit in this journey, as well. If I haven't mentioned it before, let me mention it now. Over controlling parents nurture rebellious kids. Hyper-nurturing parents breed rebellious kids. Over involved parents nurture rebellious kids. Please note, gentle reader, that this rebellion takes on many faces, and there are many tactics and strategies that are employed by kids to get what they want or to hide and get away from the perceived control.

Sadly, this behavior goes through several iterations as the child ages and even reaches adulthood. It becomes a way to get what we want by what we consider the easiest means possible. Of course, these "easy means" take so much energy for all concerned. In the long run, it is much easier to simply behave normally and ask for what you want in a mature and grown-up fashion, having patience if you don't get what you want right away. But that is too easy. Oddly enough, over time, we would find that easy and simple are good things, that they bring a sense of peace to an otherwise chaotic world. Unfortunately, like all things that work well, we will eventually quit doing it and allow the gravity of dysfunction pull us back down into the muck and mire of despair and immaturity.

So, what are these so-called self-defeating games, anyway? Here are a few examples (and the list is not exhaustive).

1. ***Throw a tantrum*** (obviously). Once again, this has its roots in our early-childhood development. As adults, this can take on various incarnations. One incarnation is to snap, to totally lose your temper, and make a complete fool of yourself. Not cool. Another incarnation of this is to play the "big, bad wolf," and "huff and puff and blow the house down." This behavior has fewer words but the behavior is unmistakable. It is like experiencing a tornado but in relative quiet. You know there is a storm going on; you know the person is totally pissed. They just aren't verbalizing things. They are, however, letting everyone know by their intensified breathing, beet red face, and veins popping, that there is something gravely amiss. If the first example is a full-on tornado, noise and destruction everywhere, then the second example is a tornado with the "mute" button engaged. Unfortunately, I am all too familiar with this second example. People would do things to me, and I wouldn't confront them, but make no mistake, they would pay. Someone would pay, and all too often it would be my family.

2. ***Pick a fight.*** Once again, anger and a lack of self-control gets the best of us. Although our behavior may be controlled (no fisticuffs involved most of the time), our anger and outrage must be satiated, and this will

be done through words and confrontation. The old adage "sticks and stones" really doesn't hold any water. Our words have such power, and with a single sentence, one can bring the utter destruction of another's spirit, especially a child or spouse. Of course, that's a coin that has two sides. On the one side, the words can bring death and destruction; the other side of the coin sees the same action, speaking words that bring abundance, confidence, and life. More on this later.

3. *Hide.* Or isolate. Many times, when we are offended or don't get what we want, we withdraw into ourselves, into our own little worlds. It is in these places that we find the breeding grounds for the lies and deceptions that the world around us would have us believe. As we learned in the "Mindfulness" section, our thoughts will, ultimately, lead to our words, actions, habits, and oftentimes, this will lead to self-destruction and utter personal chaos. And this destruction is not just self-inflicted, it affects those around us, as well. Ask the family of any substance abuser/drug addict. Ask my family.

4. *Whine and complain.* Hearing people whine and complain is like fingernails on a chalkboard (yes, I am dating myself). It sets people off, even puckers them up. It pretty much stops things in their tracks. That's when the complaining becomes the "cheese" to the whine, so to speak. Again, this is learned behavior. It starts off small and insignificant, but as we grow older, it festers into a tumor that is a blight on one's soul. It is ugly and unsightly. Unfortunately, it can be very contagious, as well. Whining begets whining and then more whining. Don't get me wrong; there are not only times to complain, there are proper ways to complain. State your case confidently, with poise and neutrality, inflecting it with passion as required. Controlled passion, most advisedly.

5. *Overcompensate.* This has become quite a thing lately. It takes on many forms, each form and iteration as destructive as the next. In many cases, overcompensation has taken on the form of full-blown substance abuse/ addiction, completely and totally ruining the individual's life and the life of their families and friends. Of course, there are other forms of overcompensation, including but not limited to sex and porn, gambling, gossiping and lying, cheating, hoarding, eating, and the list can go on. It

is important to note that, aside from eating, each of these overcompensating behaviors affect more than just the individual. Of course, it can be argued that eating affects more than just the eater, but we don't have the time to get into that here. Overcompensation serves to cover up and hide underlying conditions that, for whatever reason, we have become afraid of addressing.

As you can see, this is a non-exhaustive list. Most of us have gone through our formative years learning how to get what we want, usually by less than scrupulous means. The ends, in this case, do not justify the means. If we are not mindful of our behavior, it will lead to some seriously bad behavior, which will lead to even more bad behavior for our children. For the sake of the children, please be mindful of your behavior and make the requisite changes and adjustments accordingly and in a timely fashion, being patient with yourself if and when you fall.

Points to Ponder

1. *What self-defeating games do you play when you have been hurt or when you want to get your way?*

2. *How has this worked for you in life?*

3. *List some mature alternatives to self-defeating games.*

Chapter 20
NEGATIVE SELF-TALK
OR "TAPES"

Although I have mentioned much of this in the "Mindfulness" section, much of it bears repeating here, with some definite twists and additions. Let's begin.

I am going to refer to negative self-talk as "tapes." These are the words, phrases, and sentences that seem to play in an unending loop in our minds and even come audibly out of our mouths. This thought process and behavior begins at a very young age. It is usually brought on by those closest to us, be it a loved one, extended family member, or even a good friend or friends. It is always borne out of their own dysfunction and shortcomings. In many cases, as is the case with close family members, it is usually done "with your best interests in mind" or "you'll thank me later," especially when it comes to the crushing of the dreams and aspiration of youth.

I'm sure you've heard it said that "youth is wasted on the young." The reason for this is that, as we grow older and our bodies start to slow and break down, our minds are put to use, experiences in life turn into wisdom, and we only dream, in our wildest dreams, that "if we only knew then what we know now" things would be so different. Or to quote a famous person, "The spirit is willing, but the flesh is weak." Perhaps Benjamin Button was onto something (referring to the character played by Brad Pitt, who was born a gnarly old man and grew younger as naturally as everyone else grows older). Think of the benefits of that; the one downside being that you can't really prolong your life. Digressing, once again.

Just think, though, how much different life would be if all you received was positive feedback. This does not preclude realistic feedback done in a positive, life-giving manner. Perhaps better stated, feedback given in a positive manner. Much better. Think of how different life would be if you heard at a young age, "You can do it", rather than, "You can't do that; don't be silly." Or "That's not for people like us." How do words like those affect a young, impressionable mind, one that literally idolizes the mom or dad or older brother/sister who speaks them. What if a certain patent clerk was content with being a patent clerk? What if he'd been told for years that he was just a dreamer, to put his mind to work being a decent patent clerk, that he could one day move up in the patent office? Where would the world be without Albert Einstein? Of course, I have no idea of what he was doing for the Swiss Patent Office around the turn of the twentieth century, but I do know that he developed his "special theory of relativity" there. My point being that all he had at the time was a bachelor's degree from Swiss Federal Polytechnic and had been out of school for only two years. He recognized in himself the burning desire to explore, research, document all the thoughts that were likely burning holes in his brain trying to get out.

Or what about the young, lazy wrestler from Kentucky, who loved to "read, scribbling, writing, ciphering, writing, poetry etc.?" My real question is, how did this lazy, uneducated, kind of poor guy, after losing elections and children, and listening to all the naysayers telling him he was lazy, go on to become one of the greatest presidents in US history? We've all heard the whole story of Lincoln and his shortcomings and failures, but what if he had actually listened to and taken to heart all that excrement? Instead, he taught himself to read, write, and even become a lawyer. When asked about his learning experience and who he studied with/under, he replied, "No one."

History is full of similar types of stories, of people who DID NOT listen to the negative tapes but overcame them through the power of their dreams, beliefs, and aspirations. Tapes suck; don't believe them under any circumstance. It's been said that "God didn't make no junk" and that is true of everyone. Believe the best in yourself; not many others will. Find the ones who do and don't let them go. All we need to do is remember the story of Gideon and the tapes he was listening to and believing. "I'm a slave, the least in my father's family, and my father's family is the least in our tribe."

Why not just say, "I'm a lazy coward" and be done with it? Or "I'm content wallowing in slavery and oppression. Leave me alone and get someone else."

Speaking from experience, believing the best in yourself is one of the hardest disciplines to master. Isaac Newton actually came up with my next concept: the law of gravity (once again, tongue firmly planted in cheek). What I am getting at is this: All things seem to naturally fall into a veritable abyss, especially as it relates to our lives. The things we believe in ourselves naturally fall into negative territory. This seems to fit in nicely with our fallen nature. It takes a serious act of the will, or will-power if you will, to break out of this funk. Many find the task daunting and inevitably fail. In my forty years of adulthood (I was a late bloomer), I have found one thing to be true: Emotionally successful people realize, or are aware of, their weakness and seek a "higher power," or God as they understand Him, and seek deeper, spiritual help and guidance to make it through life without inflicting many casualties.

So, what are some examples of tapes? Personally, my go-to tape is "Why bother?" This has its roots in my formative years growing up. I was an only child for the first ten years of my life and life was good. All that attention, how could I complain? The downside was that we moved around from place to place, following my dad as he took on different sales jobs in different cities. It got so bad that I went to seven schools in five years and ten schools total. I know there are some who had it worse, but this is my story. Anyway, at each school, I needed to make new friends, to gain acceptance by whatever means. This was a tough row to hoe. Inevitably, I would get in fights almost every day after school, often with older, tougher guys. I developed, out of necessity, into a fairly decent athlete, genetics playing a large role in that. Every year, I would have to "make my bones" with another team or teams. I would have another group of teammates who I had to build trust with. It was a fair amount of work for a young kid, getting beat up by day and building trust through sports by night, many times with the same bullies. I also developed a sense of humor to cope. After our last move in the middle of junior high, I gave up trying to make friends, although some friendships came fairly naturally, geography becoming my friend. Then came senior high and a whole new group of guys. Fortunately, I found football, and although there were some decent guys on the team, I couldn't, or wouldn't, get close to any of them. In two years, I was off to Texas to go to school and play football.

Unfortunately, at that time, studies and studying were not my friends. After a decent first year of grades, they quickly tanked, and I was invited to leave, read: given the boot. So, my dreams of pro ball and a career were dashed on the rocks of "Why bother?" Its lies took me to a low-paying warehouse job.

The good news is that I eventually found someone to bother about and she even liked me. We've been married for nearly forty years and spawned two great kids and three wonderful grandsons, with a fourth grandchild en route. The bad news is that the "why bother" stigma has seemed to follow me through my career. Any time I would get successful, something would happen, and I would lose my opportunity. For example, I took a sales job for an industrial-supply company. Before I was hired, a major account of theirs went belly up. The powers that be decided that, instead of pulling back, they would be proactive and hire me to build the business back up. However, they didn't adjust the sales targets at all, so I was not getting any bonus commissions, just salary. But my competitive nature and positive attitude spurred me on. Within seven months, I had made up the 20 percent deficit in sales and the future was looking bright. I had even exceeded the old targets and was on the bonus structure. Unfortunately, my boss saw that I was making more than him and decided he wanted my job. He also knew that we had been awarded a major contract in my territory, and the news would be made public the next month. Needless to say, he found some story to tell head office, and I was canned. He took my job and made a killing the next year while I licked my emotional and financial wounds. Yes, why bother "givin' 'er" when you are just gonna get screwed anyway?

So, what to do about this kind of junk that follows you? It doesn't matter how many times you get beaten down; it matters how many times you get back up. One more story. When I was just a pup of five years old, I went to this guy's house where he and a bunch of guys were playing in the back yard. When I got there, they all piled on me and beat me up. Needless to say, I went home crying to my dad. My dad was so understanding and told me to stop crying, go back there, and if they did it again, to punch the first guy in the nose; then they'll stop. So, I marched back up, and when they saw me, they rushed me and piled on, beating me again. I went home crying, and my dad gave me the same "pep talk." I went back and the same thing happened yet again. Same outcome, but this time my dad followed me and stood outside the fence, just out of sight. Oh, I forgot to mention that the main guy's dad was a cop. I was petrified, but my dad wasn't, and he was there to make sure I did my job. As soon as I walked in, they saw me, rushed me, and when the first guy was within striking distance, I let my right-hand fly from somewhere way down behind by ankle, (read: I really wound up). My fist found the closest thing to hit: buddy's nose. It splattered, showering blood everywhere. He turned and ran to his mother, who was watching the bullying and was very upset with me. Didn't matter that I was the brunt of the bullying that her dearly beloved, yet clearly spoiled child was leading. So, I did what any self-respecting five-year-old would do: I turned and walked out to my waiting father. He wasn't smiling or anything, and I was a little nervous. We walked silently back to our house, and I was truly getting scared. When we got in our yard, he stopped me, kneeled down to my level, looked me in the eye, and said, "Now, don't you wish you would have done that to begin with?" What? My dad was advocating violence? Okay, maybe that wasn't quite what my five-year-old mind was saying. I think what I was thinking was that the kid's dad was a cop, and my dad didn't care. Whoa! I'll be okay.

So, what happened to this kid who grew up all over the countryside and couldn't be bothered with anything anymore? A number of things, and not all were good. I experienced a series of total failures in business, went through so many sales jobs that I can't remember them all. There were a couple of constants that were present in my self-destructive behavior, despite my self-destructive behavior. First, there was my unfaltering faith in God. I always knew God loved me, or at least, He tolerated me (tape!). Second, I knew my wife loved me and my kids loved me. In that respect, I was very blessed. After my last sales job fiasco, I went away on a hunting trip and took some time to journal. I wrote down what an ideal life would look like, and then when I got home, took steps to bring this to fruition. So, I took a job in law enforcement with the federal government, getting some much-needed security in employment. There was also the job satisfaction that I so desperately craved. I finally found my niche career-wise at least. There is always a way out if you just look.

So, what are some of your tapes? What are the things you say to yourself, that you tell yourself, that completely limit your behavior? Let's look at a couple of examples of the things we say to ourselves that keep us from becoming the types of people we really want to be, the types of people that we were ultimately destined to become. First, once again for me, there is the "Why bother?" tape. You can see the limiting potential in that, I am sure. Then there is "I can't do that," followed by "I am not good enough." Let's not forget "I *can* do that," which can be equally destructive. Perhaps the "Tapes" should be a subset of the previous chapter on "Self-defeating Games." Continuing on with a little humor, there is "If I didn't have bad luck, I wouldn't have any luck at all." This one usually happens after the fact, when things have gone in the crapper. This one is actually significant, because it can breed laziness. We depend on luck, so we don't plan and prepare as much as we should, and when the feces hit the oscillator, it's just bad luck. Have you ever heard the saying "You have to be lucky to be good?" It should always be followed by "You have to be good to be lucky." Or how about, "Chance favors the prepared mind?" So much for bad luck.

These are just a few of the tapes that limit us. There are many more, probably as many tapes as there are people, but the point is made. What we say to ourselves can either build us up or destroy us. Choose to be built up by your words. You are worth it.

Points to Ponder

1. *What are your main go-to tapes?*

2. *How do they hinder you from getting the best from life and relationships?*

3. *What truths can these negative tapes be replaced with?*

Chapter 21
DENIAL

I will not live in Denial (not the river in Egypt).

Those who are more geologically inclined will know that one of the characteristics of a meandering river is that the current travels faster on the outside current than on the inside. This leads to the deeper bends in the course of the river. The same is true of denial. When a situation comes up that is rather shameful, our natural inclination is to "bend" the truth. As time passes, the denials come faster and faster, until such time as the issue fades and the course corrects until the next "bend" in life. As the crow flies, a meandering river is not very long, relatively speaking. If you were to stretch the waterway out into a straight line, you would have a much different measurement.

Such is a life filled with denial. The more denial, the longer the waterway of life gets. It takes so much energy to keep up with all the lies, half-truths, and embellishments. Each one of these is like a meander in the river. So, what is denial and why is it so bad?

Well, I know there are those who think denial is terribly overrated. Actually, these people are well aware of their issues and say this facetiously. Seriously, though, denial is denying the truth about an issue to avoid the personal or public shame associated with the incident, whether real or perceived. It is always accompanied with some face saving, or even heroics to make oneself look good either personally or publicly.

How many scandals have we witnessed over the decades where the perpetrator has vehemently denied involvement of any wrongdoing? In my lifetime, I can think of a few. "The US military is not sending troops into

Cambodia;" "I am not a crook;" or my personal favorite, when Ronald Reagan was confronted in a press conference regarding the Iran-Contra issue, his response was one for the ages, "Would a nice guy like me do a thing like that?" Money in the bank, especially delivered with a smile in his folksy way. Unfortunately, in each of these cases, the truth comes out and people have to backpedal. Politics and politicians aside, lying being in their genetic code, apparently, what if we all were honest about our situations right from the get-go?

Recently (2018), accusations of sexual harassment and abuse seem to have become the rule rather than the exception. This begs the question, "Why are some men such pigs?" Well, that's a topic for another book. My real question is, "Why do some women who experience sexual harassment and abuse wait, sometimes years, to tell their story?" That I can answer, hopefully, satisfactorily.

First, there is the trauma of the event. Harassment can be every bit as traumatic as abuse. And trauma can affect some people decidedly differently than others. For our purposes here, we are going to look how the shame of the experience works. Shame can handcuff the emotions better than any police handcuff. I've seen it shut people down and shut them up completely. Unchecked, this can go on for years, festering and infecting the spirit, sometimes becoming "gangrenous," leading to self-destruction and even suicide. This is truly tragic.

Then there is guilt. I'm referring to the negative aspect of guilt, in this case (positive guilt can be a healthy warning system that something is wrong). Negative guilt blames and condemns. It minimizes the negative event, often poo-pooing it like it was nothing, even taking the blame for the action against you. If someone has offended you, confront them, in love, but confront them nevertheless. This negative guilt often lies to you by saying after you have been offended or violated that it is your fault, that you have done something wrong, hence the guilty feeling.

Time has a way of minimizing an event on its own. Time, in this case, is like gravity, allowing the negative event to sink into the depths of your spirit until you forget it even happened. Of course, no one ever forgets. It just gets covered by the sands of time. The old saying, "time heals" is generally bogus.

Time replaces pain and suffering from an ugly event with other aspects of life. There are few healing qualities with time.

There was an event on the news the other day regarding a female police officer who filed a complaint about a fellow (male) officer who was sending her crude, lewd, and socially unacceptable "correspondence" in the form of texts and emails. The police board found the male perpetrator guilty of the accusations and docked him eight hours pay. In a surprising (read: shocking) twist, they also found the female guilty and gave her the same punishment. Why? Because she waited too long to report it. Is there any wonder why this type of crap goes on when the victim is vilified as much as the offender? Waited too long. Unbelievable. As an aside, is it any wonder why trust in law enforcement is at an all-time low?

All of these things lead to denial, and denial will run its evil course in life. So, how do we stop the impending flood of denial, in keeping with our "meandering river" metaphor? Let's begin with the ABCs of "awareness/ acknowledgement, belief, confession."

1. Acknowledgement. Admitting a wrong committed against you is the first step in the healing process. This will break much of the hold that denial has on you. Becoming aware of a problem is necessary to avoiding that same problem in the future. The flip side is also true: If you become aware of a negative, hurtful behavior, don't deny that you do it. Accept it, make any necessary amends, and move on

2. Belief. This is a multi-faceted component of the healing process. First, believe that your feelings are real. An offense was committed against you that caused pain. Believe it. Then believe in the process of healing. It can be real and happen to you. Refer back to the chapter on "Forgiveness."

3. Confession. In this case, you are confessing a wrong perpetrated *against* you, not *by* you. This is oftentimes the toughest component in the process. This is where you pretty much lay yourself bare in front of your offender. You are "confessing" to them, or agreeing with what happened to you, the grief they caused you. Confession can easily be defined as agreeing with ... whatever. In this case, you are telling your story. If it is not possible or practical to confront the offender, then simply do it with yourself and/or your counselor.

Now, what if you did something that you are not proud of, either to your-self, by yourself, or against someone else? Well, follow the ABCs in the same way. Don't hold anything back; be brutally honest. Don't be afraid to take an inventory of past hurts and offenses, either by you or to you. You owe it to yourself, your family, and your friends.

Personal anecdote time, and this speaks to the power of shame to control an event. When I was ten, and we had just moved back to Calgary, Alberta, we took on a border, who happened to be a cousin (second, once removed). He was ten years older than me and was attending the local technical school, studying to be an electrician. He was so cool; we would play table hockey every day in the colder times, and he even had a motorcycle. As fate would have it, he was also sexually twisted and used the trust I had in him against me. He told me that, to be accepted as one of the guys, I had to do certain things to him. This went on for several months. Then one day, my dad and him were arguing and my dad was livid. Oddly enough, it had nothing to do with me. My cousin had lied to him and to his (cousin's) parents about something, playing both sides against the middle. When my dad told me, I thought he was overreacting, but he was firm, telling me that, with someone like that, there is always more than what meets the eye. But that was my dad, going from A to B to Z in his uncanny way.

The result of this sordid issue in my life was a complete repression of the events. It was so complete that, when I was thirty and on staff at a college in Alberta and heard the dean of students tell the male audience that he had been sexually abused as a kid, I offered a prayer of thanksgiving saying how glad I was to have never been through anything like that. Of course, the words had no sooner formed in my mind than I recalled the events from twenty years previous. Bombshell central. I was, needless to say, stunned. Guilt and shame and self-condemnation pretty much overwhelmed me. My first coherent thought was, "I have to tell my wife." And so, I did. Don't ask me why I thought to share this with anyone, but thankfully, I did. And what a burden was lifted. And such is the full nature of denial; sometimes it hides in the folds and crevices of our minds, lurking in the darkness, waiting to rear its evil head and spring its heinous trap.

I'm not sure what negative affect repressing the events had, but I am sure there are many. Don't get me wrong; I still had a lot of work ahead of me. In fact, one of the hardest issues I had to face was that of forgiveness. How do you forgive someone who so remorselessly, callously, and selfishly defiled you, someone you trusted and who betrayed that trust? It ain't easy; I'll tell you that. But one of the lessons I've learned in life is that you don't have to like it; you just have to do it. Often, this takes time and even practice. For the sake of your sanity, please work on it; you are worth it.

In closing, surround yourself with people you can trust, who can give you non-judgmental feedback about your life. They will keep you honest and true to yourself and will also keep you on the straight and narrow. Good friends are hard to come by; when you find them, don't let them go.

Points to Ponder

1. *What traumas have you experienced in your life?*

2. *What offenses have you committed, either to yourself or to others?*

3. *Have you accepted the full weight of the actions done to you or by you?*

4. *How can you make this right?*

Chapter 22
UNRESOLVED ISSUES

I will not allow issues to go unresolved in my life.

I heard a message thirty-five years ago where the speaker had committed to keep current accounts with God. This meant that he would be open and aware of his life to the extent that he would not go a single hour without making amends to whoever he offended, be it with God or someone else.

Once again, awareness is at the core of resolving issues, and where would we be without humility? After being made aware of a given issue, it takes humility to act on it, as in making amends or asking forgiveness, or both. Having mentioned these two traits, I would be remiss if I didn't mention openness and honesty, as well. For our discussion today, I will focus on openness and mention honesty at length later.

Actually, openness and humility go hand in glove. It's really hard to have one without the other. Think about it for a second. If someone is filled with pride, they are usually so self-consumed and self-absorbed that they are only open to the good points, as they perceive them, in their lives. Further to this, their inner lives are usually so fraught with denial that they hardly recognize their true selves anymore.

If, however, they open themselves to feedback—honest, constructive feedback—and humbly accept it, their lives are forever changed. Sure, it can be painful at first, but that quickly opens the door to freedom of the spirit. When they start making amends, usually first with themselves and then with others, their worlds are shaken (not stirred) so much that it could be measured on the Richter Scale. The more pride in one's life, the deeper the pain brought on by denial, and if true openness and humility are present, the deeper and more powerful the internal shaking.

When it comes to resolving issues, how exactly do we make amends? This was mentioned in the *Forgiveness* chapter, but bears repeating here. There are different schools of thought regarding this topic. Some say that you state the offense but don't ask forgiveness, yet. Not a fan of this, personally. When you open a wound like this, there really should be an end in sight. I would like to offer a suggestion in this regard. After stating how you have behaved (behaved poorly, by the way), holding nothing back, perhaps mentioning the pain caused by your behavior and the ongoing hurt that the other person has had to endure, allow them to acknowledge what you've said, perhaps acknowledge the pain suffered, all the while listening intently, "feeling" their pain. Then, after a moment, say something like, "I would like to ask you something but don't need an answer right away. Give it some thought, please. My question is this: Would you, could you, see it in your heart to forgive me? Take some time to process what I've said, and we can talk later. Thanks." My experience, and I have lots of experience being so *un*aware of my bad behavior, is that, unless there is serious abuse issues, emotional or physical, or even rape, the people have been waiting for you to say something and are happy to offer forgiveness, knowing that there is a spiritually freeing component to this act (not that I have ever even *thought* of physically abusing or raping anyone). Others may, indeed, need extra time to process the events. Give them however much time they need, you don't know how deep they have been affected. After all, this isn't about you as much as you would like to believe.

That covers resolving issues with others (big understatement of the issues, I know, as books have been written on the subject), so we will now, briefly, look at resolving issues that we may have with ourselves. Oftentimes, this is the flip side of the same coin. Again, speaking personally from experience, although I haven't felt the same pain as the pain I inflicted, I have felt the pain knowing that I caused grief in another's life. Not the same pain, for sure, but every bit as deep, requiring a different thought process in healing, but the same fundamentals are at play. And what are these fundamentals?

They are basic and have been dealt with earlier but bear mentioning here. Let's start with awareness. Being made aware of an offense committed against someone is a critical first step. After all, if you don't know you've done something it's pretty hard to make amends for it. Such is the nature of awareness. Following awareness, of course, comes humility. Swallowing your pride is such a huge part of the healing process. It makes you realize that you are not an island and don't live in a vacuum, that people aren't present in your life to serve you and be the brunt of your soundbite existence.

The next fundamental in the personal-amends process is open confession, first to yourself, and then, if your belief system allows, to God. If necessary and practical, confess to another person. This can be very cathartic, or cleansing, for your spirit. There is such a spiritual release involved in this small act that you will wonder why you waited so long, if in fact, you have waited. Then there is forgiveness of yourself. That is easier said than done. After all, how does one forgive oneself? At least, that's a question posed to me by another pastor. Giving this considerable thought, I finally came up with a fairly simple explanation. When the bible speaks of forgiveness, it refers to a legal term meaning "a pardon." In fact, as mentioned earlier, when God forgives us, he throws our sins as "far as the east is from the west." I am not sure how he does that, but apparently, he does. They are no longer held against us and are forgotten. Such is the nature of forgiveness. But how does that work when we are to forgive ourselves? Well, I'm not totally sure, but I think it starts with giving ourselves a break for the guilt and shame involved. It is fairly hypocritical of us to want to be forgiven for something we have done and then go one beating ourselves up for the same event. We want them to pardon us, but don't cut ourselves a break. Sometimes, the biggest unresolved issues continue when we knowingly allow them to live on in our minds, constantly beating ourselves up for our shortcomings.

Now, I just mentioned the word "guilt." I think it is time for a quick word on this word. For the most part, guilt has been given a bad rap in our modern, pop-psychology pseudo-culture. Why is that? Is it because it makes us feel bad? Let me state from the outset that there are two types of guilt. The good type, and obviously, the bad type.

The good type is like our early warning system. If we have done something wrong, guilt shows up and tells us that something is amiss with our behavior. Guilt then becomes like physical pain when we put our hand on the stove, or step on a sharp rock, or when we walk over sharp rocks. The pain that we experience tells us there is something wrong that will cause us discomfort. With a stove, we really should stay away. The sharp rock tells us to, perhaps, watch a little closer where we are walking with bare feet. If we are walking over sharp rocks in bare feet, the pain tells us we shouldn't run, unless we are being chased by an offended mama bear who wants to do us harm. "Good" guilt is the same type of thing. If we are even slightly aware that our behavior has hurt or offended someone, the guilt we experience should tell us to make amends and even ask forgiveness.

Bad guilt is like putting handcuffs on yourself and tightening to the point where they will leave a mark with even the slightest movement. Guilt will rear its ugly head for no reason. If we succeed, we feel guilty about it. When we do something right, we feel guilty about it. As a Canadian, I can vouch for this. We say "sorry" to almost everything. It seems to be part of our national identity. I am being facetious, sorry. If we were to look a little deeper, we would see that this bad guilt is associated often with shame. In fact, in many cases, the two words become interchangeable. To look deeper still, we can see that one shameful act can lead to a life that is racked with guilt and shame, feeling guilty and shamed about our very existence. This is extreme but the point is valid. Our decisions become subconsciously based on our guilt and shame.

If we have received forgiveness from others, then we need to respect them enough to accept it and move on. You need to cut yourself some slack, not cut some skin to shed blood, to begin the inner healing process.

What happens when we have hurt someone and they come to us with their pain from the offense we have committed? Experience has taught me some valuable lessons, not the least of which is to listen intently, make eye contact, and show respect for the hurt they are experiencing. This can't be easy for them, especially if you are a stronger personality. Show humility. Repeat their words back to them, either verbatim, if it's not that long, or give a very accurate representation of the situation, including the "trigger" words they have used to describe the hurt and pain. Please don't say you are "sorry;" sorry is a state of being, an adjective, if you will. If you are going to apologize, then do it for real, use the verb, or action word, and say, "I apologize" to convey your regret in the issue. Ask how you can make it up to them, if that's appropriate. Ask their forgiveness. The key is respect: respecting them and their pain and for the process.

Which brings me to my final point: living in peace with all around me. Another way to look at this is being free from the bondage of pain, both inflicted on others and self-inflicted. The forgiveness process is critical, as it frees you up to be you. I can't stress enough how important it is to be comfortable in your own skin. I can't imagine how I existed earlier in life, knowing that I might have caused pain in someone's life and have to look them in the eye as though nothing happened. There is redemption in the amends process, and it is a redemption that is both unburdening and freeing. We are freed from the shackles of grief that we have caused others and ourselves. Don't hesitate, make amends today, keep short accounts with yourself, with others and with God.

Points to Ponder

1. *What unresolved issues are there in your life?*

2. *How would the quality of your life improve if these issues were resolved?*

3. *What is keeping you from resolving these issues?*

4. *You may have received forgiveness from someone, but are there amends that need to be made?*

Chapter 23
MASKS

I will not wear masks to hide my true self.

It seems as though we all wear, or have worn, masks to hide who we really are. These masks are used to cover up our true selves, lest people see us for who we really are. We certainly can't have that; no one will like us or want to be around us. We will be shunned and left to our own devices, wandering aimlessly through the wilderness of life.

At least, these are the lies we tell ourselves as we don our favorite "go-to" mask. Once again, wearing masks is learned behavior, behavior that we have learned from a young age. It becomes very familiar and comfortable to put these masks on; indeed, they become an extension of ourselves. If fact, they become so familiar that we don't even realize that we are hiding behind them.

So, what do these masks look like? My go-to mask was that of humor. Moving around so much, I had to find ways to blend in, to be accepted. I learned at a very young age that kids tended to like the ones who made them laugh. I became the class clown, developing a rapier wit and becoming the scourge of teachers in two time zones, such was my skill. Of course, I also excelled at sports and my mask of humor followed me to the fields, courts, and ice rinks, becoming the scourge of coaches in two times zones. Of course, I didn't realize how difficult it was to coach when one of the kids was constantly competing with you for attention until I became a coach myself. Let me say, there is very little in life that is more frustrating than trying to keep the attention of a group of kids than talking over some smart ass who seems to think that they have something more important to say than you do. I am almost inclined to find my ex-teachers and ex-coaches and apologize for my behavior, but alas, I am not sure that they are even alive. So, former teachers and coaches, if you are reading this, please accept my humblest apologies.

One of the main things a mask will do is keep people from seeing our inadequacy, or our fears and insecurities. This was the case for me. I didn't want people to see my fear of being exposed, my fear of them getting to know that I didn't have it all together. They wouldn't like me then. I didn't want people to see my fear of losing them as friends, so I kept them at arm's length, and kept the friendships superficial. I didn't want people to see my loneliness, to see my weakness. So, on went the mask and into hiding I went, behind a mask of humor.

Let's look at some other masks people wear to hide who they really are. Please note, this is not a comprehensive list, by any stretch. It is simply here to illustrate how we try and hide who we really are.

1. *The People-Pleasing Mask.* People pleasers are conflict adverse. As a result, they do and say things that avoid any negative reactions and their identities are found in the positive responses of those they are trying to please. You will find many people who don the *people-pleaser* mask asking for advice from those they come in contact with. The result of this leads to a weak personal foundation with the person shifting between opinions like a cork on the sea. They seem to draw their worth from how well others think of them

2. *The Mask of Introversion.* I need to differentiate between someone who is introverted and someone who puts on the mask of introversion. There are introverts who simply don't get much energy from being around others; they tend to recharge in solitude, and are more comfortable being alone than being in a group. This is different than those who wear the mask of introversion. Whereas introverts can easily mingle with others, those wearing the mask can't or don't. Those wearing the mask seem to wallow in loneliness for fear of rejection

3. *The Mask of Self-Deprecation.* I am not referring to self-deprecating humor here. What I am referring to is a real sense of unworthiness. These ones seem to beat themselves up before others have a chance. They experience the self-inflicted pain of this negative self-belief instead of

letting others beat them up. Of course, others (in most cases) could care less, believing in you more than you believe in yourself, and in many cases, are offended at your self-flagellation. These ones push people away with the ugliness of this mask.

4. *The Mask of the Bully.* We all know a bully from our childhood. Unfortunately, these ones, if they are not confronted early on, grow up to be bullies. Generally insecure, they don the mask of a bully to overcompensate for their sense of insecurity, to elevate their sense of self-esteem. For some reason, they don't think social norms apply to them, and they become loud, physical, and boisterous, trying to intimidate others to follow or agree with them.

5. *Joe Cool.* This is one of the more subtle masks that people wear. They can come across as calm and collected, on the outside. On the inside, the wearers of this mask are often living at the tipping point. It doesn't take much to make them snap, and snap they do, usually at a loved one, friend, or subordinate. Those who wear this mask are usually only a step or two away from a nervous breakdown due to the fact that they keep their emotions locked up. Unless there is a release valve to vent some emotion, the emotion will find a way to get out, hence, the tipping point mentioned earlier.

As was mentioned earlier, we wear masks to hide who we really are. The mask is thought to keep others at arm's length and to not let them in to see us for who we are. I wore my mask because I didn't want anyone to see my insecurity, to see my fears and inadequacy. I wanted so much to be liked and accepted that I did things that I thought people would like. If they liked these things, they would like me. It should also be noted that, in donning the mask, it was thought that this would be a shortcut in developing relationships. If they had a reason early on to like and accept me, they would like me sooner. What I didn't realize was that the mask actually was counterproductive in developing relationships. Sure, it was better than leaving things to run their course and allowing people to actually get to *know* me.

Another issue that the masks evolved was keeping friends at arm's length because with the pattern of moving and changing schools, it eased the pain somewhat when it came to make the inevitable move. As there were no deep and meaningful bonds created, there was no pain in severing these ties. Many of the "friendships" that I made were like one-night stands. I moved into the neighborhood, got acquainted with some like-minded, athletic types, and moved on. It was as if they were "one-year stands."

The take-aways to wearing masks is simple: They are utilized, usually subconsciously, to protect us from perceived pain; they are used to hide behind and not let people see us. Masks become like walls that are erected around our souls and spirits, not letting anyone in and not letting ourselves out. Masks are best left in the closet till Halloween, when everyone is wearing them.

Points to Ponder

1. *What are some of the masks that you wear?*

2. *What is it you are trying to hide from people?*

3. *How is wearing a mask working for you?*

4. *Does wearing a mask hinder intimate relationships with others?*

Chapter 24
I WILL NOT ABDICATE PERSONAL RESPONSIBILITY

It is interesting to note, obviously, that for every "I will not" there is a corresponding "I will." In this case, "**I will not abdicate personal responsibility**" followed by "**I will take responsibility**...." They say the same thing; it is just that one is negative, and one is positive. I have counseled many over the years who have bemoaned the fact that someone near and dear to them abdicated responsibility and left them to fend for themselves. One of the great abdications of the modern era, at least in Europe and North America, was that of the British monarch King Edward VIII who decided to marry a non-British citizen and divorcee. Shocking world news, especially on the cusp of war in Europe. After all, the one to take over was the stuttering younger brother, who did not abdicate any responsibility, and indeed, overcame the double issues of being the second choice to be king, and on a more personal note, took lessons in speech to overcome his stuttering. He went on to lead Britain through the war years before succumbing to his illnesses, coronary thrombosis likely brought on by smoking, leading to his ultimate demise in February of 1952. So much for the history lesson.

The fact is, when abdicating the throne, Edward left all responsibility of the throne, of his homeland, and left for a post-war retirement in France. My point being that when one abdicates all responsibility goes with them. For a parent, this can be either devastating for the kids, with character building slowing down or stopping completely, or it can be the catalyst to inspire them to greatness and success. It is devastating, because a parental role model is lost.

Character building takes a hit in that sometimes kids step up and fill the void. Instead of the kid growing up as a child to adolescence then adulthood, he or she is thrust into the unenviable role of instant adulthood. The flip side of this is that they never grow up and remain stuck in their immaturity, growing up with very undesirable character traits. So, we have two types of kids in these situations. There are the kids who step up and take responsibility, and the kids who stay stuck. These same kids need a different type of counseling than their devastated siblings. Also, unlike their devastated siblings, they take responsibility for their issues. The devastated ones tend to live like victims, blaming Mommy or Daddy, whichever one abdicated, for all their woes in life. Please refer to the section on Victor/Victim for further clarification.

I want to touch back on a story I've already shared: the story of twin brothers who, for whatever reason, only had a mother. The mother had some serious issues and would lock the brothers in a closet or pantry. It was dark and scary and there were rats. It was a traumatizing time, to say the least. As life would have it, one of the brothers grew up with substance abuse and derelict behavior. The other grew up to be renowned in his field. When a reporter wanted to do a story about the accomplished brother, the fact that he had a derelict twin came out. The intrepid reporter did his due diligence, looked up the other brother, and heard the story first hand. The brother told him all he had gone through and concluded by saying, "After all that, I was devastated. What do you expect? I became an addict."

To follow up with his story with the accomplished brother, he confronted the brother with the sordid details as given by the "other" brother. The accomplished brother said, "After all that, I was devastated. What do you expect? I had to get out and make sure that never happened to me or my family. I went to school, studied hard, and became the best in my field."

Such is the way of abdicating one's responsibility, and such is the way of taking responsibility. One thing leads to another; a compromise is made here, morals corrupted there, and soon, you are far from where you were intended to be. How are you compromising what you know is right? Are you guilty of abdicating the responsibilities set before you? If so, what steps can be taken to get back on track? I can't stress enough the importance of living up to your responsibilities in life. This is such a critical step in the spiritual recovery process.

What does it mean to take responsibility for one's actions? Unfortunately, Hollywood has watered this down, and everyone seems to be taking responsibility for their stuff, even everyone else's stuff, hoping that their celebrity status is enough to bring about change in the world. What they fail to realize is that their celebrity status isn't enough to bring about change in their own lives, let alone the world around them. But words are cheap. What does it mean when you say one thing but do nothing about it? When there are no consequences to your bad behavior or hurtful words? Our legal system would have us believe that criminals pay for their crimes and thereby take responsibility for their crimes. That's a nice political thought, at least, but doesn't do much more than keep the prison system alive and kicking. Please don't get me wrong; there are some people who need to be locked away with the keys mysteriously lost. There are those, however, who should have any prison sentence avoided and a true rehabilitation program made mandatory. People need to learn how to take responsibility for their actions, how to make amends, how to repay their debt to society, and with the support of loved ones and their communities, learn to be contributing and responsible members of society. Indeed, it is the responsibility of the society to do whatever it takes to seek the rehabilitation of those who have committed crimes or are addicted to drugs. Locking them up and forgetting about them is a make-work program for prisons and lawyers.

Of course, criminals taking responsibility for their actions is at the far end of the spectrum. Most of us don't need to commit any crimes to be offensive and take responsibility for our behavior and/or words. In fact, some of us are quite gifted in being offensive. So, what are we to do? What is the point of taking responsibility for our stuff? It is my contention that taking responsibility actually brings about reconciliation in relationships, not to mention redemption. Reconciling is one thing, but what does it mean to be redeemed? The word "redeemed" was made popular in the New Testament of the Bible and refers to transactions made in the market, oftentimes referring to slaves who were bought and set free. The ramifications of this are significant. What happens when we offend someone with our actions or words is that it begins to feel like we are in bondage, somehow. Think back to the "backpack" illustration. Or when we are offended by someone; same thing. Taking responsibility for our actions (or actions that were taken against us) has a redemptive quality about it. For example, it has been said that, if you owe someone, then go to them, reconcile the debt, and you will be free. In today's credit-based society, this can be challenging. But what if what was meant was that the debt we have is emotional or psychological, then that makes things more manageable, at least from a financial standpoint. Redemption then becomes a very spiritual event. And such is the nature of taking responsibility for our stuff.

Points to Ponder

1. *In which areas of your life have you abdicated responsibility?*

2. *How can you take responsibility in these areas?*

3. *How has abdicating responsibility affected relationships?*

4. *How would these relationships look if responsibility for your actions and/or words was taken?*

CHARACTER TRAITS I <u>WILL</u> EMBRACE

I am going to finish with some very basic inner, spiritual traits that we don't often think of. These are spiritual attributes that I am going to pursue, because—like Jack Nicholson's character in the movie *As Good as It Gets*—I want to be a better man. I am going to speak personally here, that it behooves me to be the best version of me possible. That being the case, I am going to live in such a way as to not be offensive, to be mostly tolerant, and to be at peace with myself and with others. Allow me to explain. The "not be offensive" part is fairly self-explanatory. I don't want to be a difficult person. By "mostly tolerant," what I mean is that I have standards, beliefs, and convictions that I will not compromise on. If you want to have different standards and beliefs, fine. We can still get along and agree to disagree. If you ask me what I think, I will tell you in a mature and respectable manner. This is also the part that relates to being "at peace with myself and with others."

Chapter 25
CHARACTER

I have said it before, and I'll say it again:
I will have character, not be a character.

Character. Why is so much made of this inner human trait? Why am I making so much of this inner trait? What are the intrinsic qualities of character that make it so elusive to some and yet second nature to others? How is character developed? So many questions, so little time. Back in the day (read: Ancient Greece), much was made of a man's virtue, or the intrinsic qualities that made him a "good" man. A few of these qualities will be discussed further as I close out the book. Suffice to say, qualities such as honesty, truthfulness, faithfulness, and loyalty, to name but a few, were highly sought out and nurtured. So, for the purposes of our discussion here, character will be used as an introduction to the other more specific qualities.

It is interesting to note that, so often, character is developed in the refining fire of trials and failure. In fact, it has been said that character is much more valuable than gold, though gold is purified by fire. You see, when gold is found in its natural state, it often has impurities found within it. In order to get these impurities out, the gold is placed in a fire, and the heat is turned up. Not just turned up but (back in the ancient days) the refiner actually had a large bellows to blow in air, thereby heating the gold to a melting point of 1064 degrees Celsius, or 1947 degrees Fahrenheit. That's pretty warm, and yet, that's how some of the trials we face have been described. And why?

Because our faith has greater worth than gold. At over USD1500 per ounce, that becomes even more significant.

So, how can we describe character? Spiritual character? First things first. If we are serious about developing our spiritual lives and doing this through developing character, it is essential that we are diligent in our pursuit of this spiritual trait. Refer back to the chapter on "Mindfulness." The following is a list of "steps" or building blocks that can be developed to achieve this.

Virtue. Virtue has been defined as a "behavior showing high moral standards." Of course, these moral standards can change with time and through cultural evolution. The Ancient Greeks were big on virtue, with Aristotle introducing twelve virtues. To Aristotle, moral virtues were acquired through practice and habit. Clearly, virtue did not come naturally and had to be worked at. In fact, it can be said that virtue, and becoming virtuous, takes spiritual discipline, conscious effort, commitment, and diligence. Virtue is foundational for developing spiritual character.

Knowledge. Why is knowledge included on this list? In today's modern culture, it would seem as though critical thinking is a thing of the past. This is due to the lack of knowledge that we have generally accumulated. It is unfortunate what has become of our education system here in the west. It seems that we don't teach things that are relevant anymore. We are stuck in an antiquated system, teaching antiquated concepts to a modern breed of child. Square peg in a round hole. It would seem that we would be better served teaching the basics of what makes our countries tick, our constitutions, the rule of law, and proper thought processes in making a cogent and lucid argument. In short, teaching kids how to think rather than indoctrinating them. In fact, perhaps it is the pursuit of knowledge of the truth that puts this character trait on our list.

Self-Control. This certainly is an attribute worthy of our list. I have found, coming out of the life of addiction that I led for 6.75 years, that I have much more self-control now than I had *before* I plunged into the depths of homelessness and addiction. I have more self-control in most areas of my life, except in one notable and very significant area. Being homeless for those six plus years, I wasn't doing much driving. As a result, I seemed to have forgotten how people drive. Like the bumper sticker says, "It's not the ups and downs that bother me when I drive; it's the jerks." I don't recall there being so many jerks, of which I am certainly one—at least while driving. This is one area in which I definitely need to work on my self-control. Not to be accepting of the bad driving habits of others but at least to be tolerant of them. My anger levels should be brought into check, my blood pressure levels should be managed better, and the overall temperature in the car should be lower. But driving analogies are a dime a dozen. Sure, they are easy and most everyone has issues when driving. There are, however, other areas in life that require self-control. Here are a few areas worth considering:

1. *Gambling.* There is nothing wrong with gambling, when done in moderation. It can be fun and entertaining; you may even win, though there are usually two chances of that, and slim just left town. The problem comes when we lose and then start "chasing" the losses, meaning we begin to throw more and more money on the same bet, hoping to recoup our losses. We go home broke, thinking of new and better strategies to win next time. And then we are hooked. Self-control would have us set a "limit and play within it." When that threshold is met, quit, walk away, leave. Whatever it takes to maintain self-control.

2. *Alcohol.* Again, nothing wrong with a little alcohol. In the Bible, Paul tells Timothy to drink some wine for his stomach. The Bible also speaks against too much consumption leading to drunkenness. Getting drunk leads to a lack of, or loss of, control. We lose control of our motor skills, our cognitive skills, and we get in the position of hurting ourselves or others by our words and/or behavior. Once again, set a limit on how much you will drink and over how long a time. Stick to it and maintain your self-control.

3. *Sex/Pornography.* Although sex can be a wonderful encounter between a man and wife, if it is misused and abused, it can lead to the destruction of lives and relationships. Often, at the root of an affair or the breakdown of a relationship, is porn. Books have been written about the emotional, psychological, and spiritual devastation brought on by the onset of porn in someone's life. Of course, the lack of self-control with porn will likely lead to a sex addiction/porn addiction. Like any addiction, this will not be healthy. Indeed, it can lead down some very dark and painful paths.

4. *Our words.* Our tongues, though very small, are in fact very powerful. Of course, I don't mean the tongue itself but the words that come out of our mouths. Why is the tongue so hard to control? Once again, the tongue can be used for good, or for evil. It can be used to build up or to destroy.

5. *Food.* Once again, food is something that is very pleasant, indeed necessary for basic human sustenance. It is the over-indulgence of food that leads to negative issues, such as obesity, Type 2 Diabetes, allergies, etc.

I am not going to mention drugs in the area of self-control simply because most drug addicts have already lost most self-control. Of course, I am speaking from experience here. Where I went through the first fifty-two years of life "saying no to drugs," never smoking pot, let alone anything harder, after getting a taste of pain meds along with the accompanying boredom and self-isolation, all my discipline, beliefs, and self-control went out the window.

Self-control, by its very nature, follows knowledge mainly due to the fact that, if we have all the facts regarding a specific issue, we will generally be less likely to fly off the handle. It would seem that knowledge breeds self-control. It would also seem that self-control breeds knowledge. If we allow ourselves time to process issues and to gain all the facts (knowledge), we find ourselves in a win/win situation. This definitely runs contrary to our fast-food, sound-bite, instant-gratification society.

Perseverance. It is interesting how perseverance follows self-control. The implication here is that many of us (read: me) often aren't as self-controlled as we would like to be. Perseverance comes into play after those times that we slip up in the area of self-control and our behavior is less than controlled. In some cases, our behavior may be out of control. In these cases, it is our loved ones who persevere on our behalf. It is during times that seem the most hopeless and lost that our persevering will yield the best fruit.

What does *perseverance* mean in this context? It would seem to be a stronger word for *endurance*. Where *endurance* may have a passive component to it, *perseverance* has a more active component, a more mindful and aware component, if you will. I look at *perseverance* this way: that when something happens that we are not expecting, we acknowledge it, put our heads down, and overcome it, knowing full well that this overcoming process may take some time to accomplish.

In developing deep, spiritual character, the presence and development of perseverance is essential. Life will be fraught with failure, challenges, and missteps. Diligently persevering through these setbacks will enable the streams of character to run deep.

Love. I have already devoted a chapter to *love* so will only spend a short time on it here. Love embodies so much of what spiritual character should be: humility, grace, kindness, patience. Love is very accepting, indeed, tolerant. But love is also true to itself and what it knows to be right. Love is adaptable but non-conformist. If we get *love* right, we will be well on our way to living a rich, spiritual life.

Character is usually not something that comes naturally to us. BEING a character is far easier, but that is something we could do without. There seem to be far too many "characters" around and not enough people *of* character. A current enigma, in my mind, is the current US President Donald Trump. An enigma, because when you look at what he has actually done, WOW. Unfortunately, and this is the enigma, he uses words to communicate and many of these words are better left unsaid. Don't get me wrong; not ALL of what he says is bad, but when he gets going it can be like listening to a bully in an elementary school playground. And such are the vagaries of wealth and power.

Back to having character. One of the lessons I learned early on in my career was taught to me by one of the most spiritual people I have ever known. She was the wife of our senior pastor and told me that the issue was never the issue. Often, when counseling people, I found this to be the case. They would come with deep-seated problems but be content to jump around the real, underlying issue, afraid of revealing what was really bothering them. They would hide behind many different masks, some of which included humor, tears, and of course, the mask of denial. Every now and then, one person would open up honestly about what was really, truly bothering them. I would question myself regarding this, because that type of honesty was so rare. Why? Surely, I had enough discernment to see honesty in someone, as opposed to constantly reading and wading through the lies. Such is the difficulty in practicing character. Too many painful issues to wade through, too much to protect yourself from. The good news is that it can be done. It will take a firm resolve deep within yourself, but it is possible.

What discussion about character would be complete without mentioning humility? A cornerstone of spiritual character is humility and humility of spirit. I have mentioned humility so much in this book that, perhaps, the title should include it. To reiterate, humility is not only looking out for your own interests, but also the interests of others. Humility leads us to serve others as we look out for their needs and interests. It has been said, and will be said again, that humility is *not thinking less of yourself but thinking of yourself less.*

Points to Ponder

1. *How would you rate* virtue *in your life?*

2. *How could you become more virtuous?*

3. *What do you do with knowledge and wisdom? Do you keep it to yourself, locked away for personal use?*

4. *What areas of your life could use a little more self-control?*

Chapter 26
HONESTY

I will be honest with my words and in my actions

I know what you are thinking: *Why isn't he talking about humility as a cornerstone of character?* Well, I am pretty sure you have firmly ingrained my thinking and the value I place on humility in your spirit. Time to move on.

Honestly, there is so much to say about honesty. Where to begin? There are some basics about honesty that can't be ignored, but it's almost a "chicken or the egg" scenario. For example, trustworthiness. Are we trustworthy because we are honest, or honest because we are trustworthy? I'm thinking the former, in this case. Honesty comes from within and is manifested internally, then externally. Trustworthiness is external; others trust us because we have proven ourselves to be trustworthy. Trust has to be earned and that begins with people knowing you are honest. Why is this so? Why not simply trust someone before they have to go through all the hoops of proving themselves to you? I will trust everyone, until they *earn* my mistrust. Being truthful definitely is a subset of honesty—being honest with your words. Integrity has to do with being honest with yourself, and true to your beliefs and actions, especially when alone. More on these later.

Being honest, or living an honest life, definitely includes all of the above, but there are at least as many negatives regarding honesty as those positive traits listed above. We shouldn't lie, cheat, steal, or do anything that we would be offended by if it were done to us. The golden rule comes to mind: "Do unto others as you would have them do unto you." Of course, there are those who pervert this by saying, "Do unto others *before* they do unto you."

Needless to say, I will be focusing more on the precepts involved with the "first" golden rule.

So, honesty is as much about being and doing good and virtuous acts as it is about NOT doing evil and wicked acts.

Where does honesty begin? It seems to be a no-brainer: with us. Honesty begins within. We need to be honest with ourselves before we can be truly honest with anyone else. I'm not even going to get into being honest with God, after all, how do we truly expect to deceive the all-knowing Almighty when he knows our every thought and feeling? Enough said. Being honest with ourselves actually precludes any thought or belief of denial. It's impossible for the two to exist together. Period. In fact, honesty with ourselves is liberating beyond description. The burdens that we carry are like the proverbial backpack filled with huge bricks. Each brick is like a lie we tell ourselves, or how we've minimized events, embellished events, or even denied events. You can see how the pack would begin to weigh you down. Being honest with yourself takes the bricks out of your pack and greatly lightens your proverbial load.

In many cases, honesty with yourself begins with personal confession. This takes the form of admitting and agreeing with yourself regarding the events that have taken place in your life. It means articulating exactly how you feel, or are feeling, about said events. Then the key is to honestly deal with everything above. A course of action may be required. Take time to think this through. After all, we don't want to go into any situation blind, leaving a wake of destruction in our path. The goal of any honest confrontation, with ourselves or others, should always be that of edification, or the building up of yourself or the other person. I am referring here to basic life conflicts that both get brushed aside or denied altogether. Things that we all experience in one way or another (although, even the painful, life-changing events should, ultimately, have the same goal of edification). Unfortunately, many of us think that the weight on our back is like an exercise, designed to build muscle. Fact is, this weight does develop "spiritual muscle," but it is the deforming and debilitating that makes us look less than desirable, figuratively speaking. In a non-politically correct world, I would say it makes us look ugly. Being honest here. There is nothing virtuous about dishonesty in any way, shape, or form.

This leads to the discussion regarding interpersonal relationships and the role of honesty within them. A few years back, there was a popular TV show called, *Lie to Me*, starring Tim Roth and Kelli Williams, among others. One of the characters practiced what he called "radical honesty." Most of the time. Anyway, the point of all this is to say that within relationships, radical honesty is not necessarily recommended. Am I advocating telling white lies that will gloss over issues and make the other person feel better about themselves? Not at all. What I am saying is that, perhaps, there are things better left unsaid. This would fall under the "choose your battles wisely" category. For example, do I agree with my wife's parenting or grandparenting skills. For the most part, yes. There are, however, some skills that I don't necessarily track with. I am not even going to mention my parenting and grandparenting skills. Suffice to say, I have learned the art of asking my adult children for forgiveness for my behavior as a parent. Is it imperative that I honestly share my feelings on this? Not hardly, and I speak from years of experience (arguing with Momma Bear is not conducive to a long and healthy marriage), hardship, tension, and mistrust. I would much rather be happy than right. Does that mean I never share my true, honest feelings with her? Once again, I choose my battles wisely. I've actually become quite adept at looking at the big picture and playing the long game in relationships. That has come at the expense of my thick, rich, brown hair, which has not only receded of late but has returned to the blond of my youth, or as some have corrected me, the gray of my old age.

Allow me to share an interesting personal anecdote about choosing your battles wisely. Consider this a little rabbit trail. We were in church recently and had our two-year-old grandson with us. At the end of the service, he likes to run around and ultimately makes his way up the wheelchair ramp to the stage. The stage is around two feet above the floor, so not too high. Well, the grandson ran up on the stage, ran to the middle, and right up to the edge, where he wanted to jump off. No big deal. I was watching him from the front row (he is too fast to follow everywhere, so I monitor him from a distance). He looked at me, and I encouraged him to go for it. He did and stuck the landing. He loved it, ran around to the ramp, across the stage, and did it again. The third time, as fate would have it, as he was getting close to the edge, he tripped over one of the designs in the carpet, fell, rolled over, and right off the stage, landing on his back. His head did not make contact. The shock "jerked the slack" out of his happy demeanor and he started to cry. No big deal, except that Grandma saw this as well. Apparently, I didn't move quick enough, and she began the angry march towards me to chastise me vehemently and comfort the little guy. Okay, seeing her out of the corner of my eye, I snapped to it. I picked him up, gave him a little hug, took him to the stage, and encouraged him to jump off again. He stopped crying, looked up at me, and got ready for launch. And launch he did. Stuck the landing, and Grandpa cheered him on.

I then "noticed" my wife, feigning ignorance of her presence and anger. I was in no mood for a tongue lashing, being told how calloused I was, how it wasn't my place to make him tough, that he hurt himself and needed some love and tenderness, all of which were inevitably en route and true in their own right. Fortunately, she saw the little guy's exuberance, and chilled considerably. To her credit, she "got" the lesson I was trying to teach: the old "if you get bucked off your horse, get right back on" lesson.

Did I feel guilty for the minor dishonesty? Yup. We had a fun talk about it when we got home. It is important to note that I did not try and justify anything but rather took ownership of it, confessing my behavior and motivation (self-preservation notwithstanding), made light of the fear of being vehemently chastised and facing the irreparable damage that would inevitably ensue, tongue firmly in cheek. The key here was to come clean. The good news is that we can be honest with one another and share our feelings, fears, hopes, and dreams. This honesty between my wife and I has been cultivated over decades of relationship failures and successes. We have developed an emotional honesty where we each know that the other loves us, where we can share our deepest emotions and concerns honestly and know that we will be fine.

A quick reminder: Having said all that regarding emotional honesty, it is not something that comes naturally. It has taken work and practice. Speaking personally, I have had to swallow my ego and my pride and listen to my wife's concerns. Often, neither of our emotions were accurate, but they were certainly real. What do I mean by this? Often, our emotional response will be based on incomplete or incorrect data. We will misunderstand the situation or motivation of the other person. This will illicit an incorrect emotional response. The response, however incorrect, is very real, based on the current understanding of the situation or event. This is where emotional honesty and emotional trust come into play. This is also where true love comes into play. If love believes the best in one another, then behavior that is out of character should be clarified and dealt with. It should be done with love and humility, knowing full well that the behavior in question may well have been misunderstood. Regardless, the negative emotion or belief needs to addressed.

Emotional honesty is one of the toughest areas to master. It is so easy to hide, and we revert back to primal behavior when our emotional connections feel threatened. This primal behavior is manifested in various ways. Depending on the severity of our emotional disconnect and the emotional conflict we are facing, we can access our flight or fight mechanism from which not much good will come. I want to add another component to the flight or fight system, and that is *freeze*. Think "deer in the headlights", or as one person I know put it, "the deer in the taillights." The *freeze* occurs in various life situations of high stress and trauma. After it happens once, the occurrence of this phenomenon reoccurs with greater frequency. We need to be honest with ourselves and our loved ones to overcome the trauma and distress. When emotional conflict occurs in a relationship, there are always at least two who are affected. This being said, we must remember that they, like you, are acting out their worst fears, and that fear is of losing their emotional connection. Remember, too, that we will always disagree with those we are close to. It behooves us to be both patient and honest with one another, lowering our expectations, and thereby lowering the level of disappointment when issues arise.

Such are the vagaries of life and relationships. There are always people who we are going to disagree with, who are going to rub us the wrong way. The spiritual key here is to honestly convey your feelings to yourself, or with yourself, ask yourself why you feel this way, and if necessary, deal with the outcome personally, or with a trusted friend. Then, if you feel strongly about it, and it fits into your big picture, lovingly, but firmly and honestly, confront the offending party. Just remember to keep edification and reconciliation at the fore. It's always better to win a friend than to lose one.

Points to Ponder

1. *What is the main area of your life in which you need to be honest?*

2. *What fears are keeping you from being honest with others and with yourself?*

3. *Is a lack of honesty keeping you from being a more trustworthy person?*

Chapter 27
TRUTHFULNESS

I will be true to myself and to my word. I will speak
the truth in love if confronted or if confronting.

Since we have established that truthfulness is the "egg" to honesty's "chicken,"
let's crack it open and see what's comes out, shall we?

If truthfulness is rooted in honesty, why even mention it? Like I said
earlier, truthfulness, for all intents and purposes, has to do specifically with
our words. I can't stress enough how vital truthfulness is in today's soundbite
society. With the advent of the concept of fake news, who do we believe?
Where is Walter Cronkite when we really need him? Actually, it was more the
era than the man, where integrity in journalism meant something, and was
an ideal to strive for. My point is that there are many competing factions for
the "truth," real or perceived. Truth has become such a relative term, not the
"absolute" that was present in a bygone generation.

It is very difficult to maintain a truthful state when everyone from our
political leaders on down are living, breathing purveyors of deception. Where
is this rooted? Well, we only need to look at the "big three" evils in life.
No, not sex, drugs, and rock and roll. I'm talking about money, sex, and
power. It is this inherent greed and insatiable lust for more that seems to
compel people to check their morals and ethics at the door. Nixon said, "I
am not a crook" but did some seriously crooked things that led to the first
resignation of a US president in modern history. But poor old Nixon wasn't
the only crooked politician to grace us in the past half century. Not even my

hero, Ronald Reagan, was blameless. Bush forty-one famously stated, "Read my lips, no new taxes," then promptly raised and added more. Clinton "did not have sexual relations with that woman," and Bush forty-three "found" WMDs in Iraq. This section isn't long enough to get into the deceptions of Obama, Hilary, or even the Donald. My point is that power corrupts and absolute power corrupts absolutely, or so the saying goes.

It would seem that both money and sex are totally linked to power and its deceptive lure into deception and lies. So why isn't the term "half-truth" used? Seriously? Probably for the same reason that courts want the "truth, the whole truth, and nothing but the truth." When it comes to truth, why do people tend to gravitate so close to the line of deception that one foot is on the truth side and one … isn't?

I remember an old guy once told me about his two children: the one would tell stories and lies because they could be told; the other would rather go to jail than tell anything other than the whole truth. Well, that's fairly refreshing. Definitely the exception rather than the rule. It does show, however, that it is indeed possible to be truthful and honest in all you say and do. Author Dan Ariely, in his 2012 book, *The (honest) Truth about Dishonesty*, had research backing up the fact that we "fudge" the truth about 10 percent or so. We tend to cheat more when we can justify it, when we see others doing it and getting away with it (lemmings that we are), although, we do it less when we are reminded to be honest. There is such power in words. We tend to lose moral authority in what we say when we are less than honest, but conversely, gain moral authority when we are truthful. I like the saying, "Everybody wants the truth, but no one wants to be honest," though I'm not sure where I first heard it.

I would be remiss if I didn't mention the social-media connection in relation to truthfulness and honesty. Data scientist Dr. Seth Stephens-Davidowitz, in his book *Everybody Lies,* looks at the seeming dichotomy between our social-media selves and reality. Maybe the dichotomy wasn't so "seeming" after all. How many of us post anything at all about what we are really feeling? Or about the misery that seems to make up our inner lives? Maybe it should be called "Fakebook" instead. How many cries for help have you ever heard on social media out of the thousands of posts every day? If you read between the lines, those cries are out there. Everybody wants the truth, but no one wants to be honest. It's almost become socially unacceptable to display any weakness whatsoever. Yet, if we are honest, it is the admission of that very weakness that can, ultimately, exude such strength of character.

Time to backtrack just a tad. I am not advocating posting all your woes on Facebook or Instagram. Not by any stretch. I am, however, advocating some moderation in our Pollyanna approach to social media. By this, I mean that we would be better served if we did not post everything that was right about our worlds as though that was all we were. Who wouldn't like to live that fairy-tale life? It's just not real. I have thought of posting something like this, "I am only going to post what is good and right in my life, in order for you to envy me, and be jealous of me, so that I can get more friends and people will look up to me." Needless to say, that never got posted, and in the spirit of truth and honesty, I pulled WAY back from social media altogether. I know my issues, and I share them with select friends whom I trust. It's not, nor should it be, up for public dissemination. Neither should my embellishments about myself. After all, anyone who knows me is well aware of my shortcomings, myriad that they are.

One last word on the benefits of being truthful. A study conducted by the University of Notre Dame in South Bend, Indiana, looked at two groups: a control group and a group that committed to telling the truth and being honest for ten weeks. Not surprisingly, the "truthful" group had fewer physical ailments (like headaches) and mental-health complaints (like symptoms of depression) than did the control group. So, if you want to improve your physical and mental-health state even a little, try being honest and truthful[3].

In conclusion, I want to reiterate that being honest and truthful in what you say not only develops character but gives you a moral authority that few today possess. Try to avoid phrases like, "to be perfectly honest with you…" for the simple fact that people will begin to question how much of what you have said previously wasn't perfectly honest. Quite simply, let your lives and words speak for themselves, without embellishment. As was mentioned earlier, words have power—power to build or power to destroy. They are like a fire, with the ability to heat, cook, and provide beauty, or lay waste to all it comes in contact with. How you use your words will

....

3   Much of what was cited here came from an article by Judi Ketteler in the NY Times.

determine your course in life. Choose them wisely. Live a healthy life filled with truthfulness.

Points to Ponder

1. *The obvious question is this: What lies do we tell ourselves?*

2. *Followed by: Why do we not only tell these lies but listen to them?*

3. *How would our lives be enhanced by being truthful with ourselves and with others?*

4. *What is it about being truthful that we are afraid of?*

Chapter 28
INTEGRITY

INTEGRITY: My thoughts, words, and behavior
will be congruent, regardless of where I am or
who I am with, especially if I am alone.

Integrity is a word that many avoid because of the implications associated with it. In this section, I want to focus on the importance of congruency in all that we do. What do I mean by that? Well, in math, specifically geometry, congruency occurs when a shape or angle is the exact same as a corresponding shape or angle. In psycho-emotional speak, congruency occurs when what we say is the same whether or not we are alone or in public, *and* what we say is the same as what we do, whether alone or in public. It is so easy to say one thing and do another. Think politicians. Or say something to someone but not believe what you say is true or do something that is contrary to what you say. It fits into the old saying of "do as I say, not as I do." We certainly live in a people-pleasing culture, so it is very easy, and simple, to brush people off by saying what they want to hear. With practice, we can get quite good at it. Trust me, some do practice this type of deceptive, incongruent behavior.

In order to determine what integrity is, perhaps we should look at what it isn't by examining some popular misconceptions. First, there is the "just be honest" thought. Although honesty is an admirable virtue in and of itself, there is more to integrity than just honesty, not to mention the overuse and abuse of the word *just*. Make no mistake, without honesty, there is no integrity. It is the "only-ness" of the word "just" that throws a wrench into the whole deal. Of course, the word *just* has become one of the most abused words in the English language. "We are *just* friends." "I was *just* being honest." "I just, I just, I just…." And the list can go on ad nauseam.

Second, there is the thought of living a balanced and compartmentalized life. These are actually two cool-sounding concepts that, when examined carefully, kinda suck. When I think of balance as a personal characteristic, I envision my two feet in buckets of water, one extremely hot and one extremely cold. Somewhere around my midline, I should be just right. Forget the scalding burns on my one foot or the frostbite on my other. So much for balance. As for compartmentalization, in some respects, I think this has been given a bad wrap, though not as it relates to integrity. I say a bad wrap, because many people use this as an excuse for poor behavior. I am thinking of people who act and speak one way at work, and when they get home, they put on good behavior and act almost saintly. On the other hand, having experienced life from a law-enforcement perspective and often dealing with the less-than-desirable elements of society, it became imperative to compartmentalize somewhat. I mean, was I going to treat my kids like criminals? What I found was that the opposite was somewhat true: I began to treat the criminals like my kids. The real compartmentalization came in when I would leave the inner stress of the job, on the job, or at the job. There is nothing wrong with that, if your behavior can remain congruent. Really, why bring unwanted stress home with you? Maybe that's why the divorce rate among law enforcers is so high: the inability to separate the job from home.

Third, there is the "it's just who you are" fallacy. There is that word "just" again. It may well be who you are, but this lacks the intentionality that is so desperately needed for integrity. What do I mean by this? Integrity has to be a conscious choice in order to be congruent with our lifestyle. Without intentionality, we can be flying by the seat of our pants. Another lesson I've learned in my long and somewhat sordid career is that Newton's Law of Gravity applies to personality traits as well as material objects. What I mean by this is that, left to our own devices, not being intentional will generally lead to a less-than-stellar lifestyle, read: disastrous, falling to unimaginable depths by the sheer force of *gravity*.

The word integrity comes from the Latin word, "integer," which means "whole and complete." It is truly a virtue to be aspired to. It refers to lacking nothing as it relates to character. The "wholeness" concept refers to all aspects of your life.

To practice integrity requires certain personality traits that take some work to master. Of course, humility is at the core of integrity, and by now you all know how I value humility. Another trait we have discussed is awareness. A brief word on this: We began our steps with "mindfulness" and have, for the most part, built on this throughout. It is critical to our spiritual growth that we be aware of all that we do and say, and that this lines up in public and private. But there are other traits that are required to practice integrity. The first one I want to discuss is self-confidence. Self-confidence, simply put, is being comfortable in your own skin and not being afraid to show it. Self-confident people aren't afraid to be themselves in most, if not all, situations. This doesn't mean they have a license to be jerks, after all, humility is at their core. It does mean that they are free to express themselves in a manner they deem prudent for the setting. It may mean simply keeping their mouth shut. Add this to "honesty" and "truthfulness" and you have the beginnings of a heretofore unrecognizable life change, for the good, I might add.

Another trait I associate with integrity and its incumbent congruency is discernment. Discernment, for our discussion here, can best be described as the ability to know what to say, when to say it, and how to say it, if we say it at all. It also describes the ability to know what to do, when to do it, and how to do it, if we do it at all. It should actually be looked at as a gift, such is the nature and value of discernment. Rare are the people today who use this trait effectively. I should note at this time that the discerning, spiritual person will know, or at least have a good idea, when others are being less than forthcoming with them. Discernment will also guide them on the best route to handling the given situation as it arises.

One last thought on integrity for our discussion (though not the last thought, by any stretch): purpose. What does it mean, exactly, as it relates to integrity? Well, purpose naturally assumes intentionality. When we have purpose in our lives, when we are actually living on purpose, then we have the foundation partly laid in living a life of integrity with intentionality. Purpose-driven lives can be game changers in the world. Purpose also implies focus and this focus of purpose needs to be multi-faceted. Purpose in career, purpose in words, and actions congruent with our entire lives, purpose in relationships, and purpose in parenting are some of the areas that are essential for a purpose-driven life of integrity. From a spiritual standpoint, there doesn't seem to be much point in living a purpose-driven life if it is not built on a foundation of personal integrity.

To conclude, integrity requires humility, congruency, discernment, intentionality, and purpose to make you both whole and complete in the life you have chosen. Strive to master all of these quietly and humbly, and you will see many positive changes in your life.

Points to Ponder

1. *Is your life congruent? Does your talk match your walk? If not, how do you change that?*

2. *Is your life lacking integrity? If so, what steps can you take to add integrity to your life?*

3. *Do you exercise patience when the situation demands discernment? Or is flying off the handle standard fare? If so, how do you change that?*

Chapter 29
HONOR

I will endeavor to act honorably always, being mindful of doing things right and doing the right thing. I will treat people with dignity and be dignified in my thoughts, words, and actions.

Honor. Now here is a word we don't hear very often. It's almost as though it has been forgotten. The concept of honor also seems to have been "misplaced." How are we going to define honor? Honor can be defined as "worthy of respect, having or showing good moral character and honesty, fair and proper." I would like to think of honor as doing things the right way honestly, saying the right things honestly, and doing the right thing with no reservations. Further, I would suggest that honor and integrity go hand in hand, as one pretty much defines the other. For some reason though, I seem to think that honor is a deeper spiritual concept. Sophocles said, "Honor isn't about making the right choices but dealing with the consequences." Leonardo da Vinci states, "Who sows virtue reaps honor." Calvin Coolidge said, "No person was ever honored for what was received. They were honored for what they gave." And how about, "Honor is not the appendage of any social class. It is a way of life freely chosen by any man or woman, regardless of race, color, or creed." T. Braxton Woody. Notice, if you will, the intentionality involved with these quotes. Making choices, dealing with consequences, sowing, giving … all of these require an act of the will.

Experience has taught me that honorable living is an experience that begins deep within our spirits, but unlike gravity, it rises to the top, not unlike cream rising to the top. It's like we have all been given a flawed canvass to draw our lives out on. There is a real ugly base coat to begin with, and it is our life's mission to turn that ugliness into a thing of beauty. How beautiful is totally up to us.

When doing a search online of stories about honor, it was shocking how many stories involved service men and women and their time "in country" in the line of duty. What happened to average, everyday people doing extraordinarily honorable things? Granted, bravery and courage are traits of honor and that is manifested by those in uniform. But what about the guy who jumps on the subway tracks to save someone? Or the girl who comes to the defense of someone being bullied, putting herself at risk of bullying and harassment? What about the kid who risks everything to save the family dog? Or the brother who gladly donates a kidney to his brother in need? These are examples of doing the right thing at the right time. Honorable things that define who we are, painting something beautiful on the canvas of our lives.

That brings us to the "dignity" part of our discussion. The word "dignity" is an oft-misused word that needs some clarifcation. Or maybe it's us who need the guidance. Be that as it may, here are some thoughts on dignity:

1. Dignity has to do with value. This means valuing both yourself and others. Needless to say, this requires humility, especially when valuing others.

2. Self-esteem. If you want to be treated differently, or better, begin to act like you are worthy of this type of treatment. Believe in yourself. Be humble.

3. Believe in others. If you think yourself better than others, it's going to be hard for them to relate to you. After all, who wants to voluntarily be around someone with a superiority complex? Way too tedious. Believe the best in others and esteem them at least as highly as you, if not higher.

4. Respect. You need to respect yourself before you can truly respect others. That means no more tapes (negative self-talk), no more self-defeating games, no more behaving badly and thinking you're okay. Start doing

things that are worthy of respect and start respecting yourself. As for respecting others, it has been said that respect has to be earned. What if it was freely given to begin with? What if everyone you came in contact with, in a relationship of any kind, started with a "full tank" of respect for them? Let them earn your *disrespect* with bad behavior or bad words. Let them know, respectfully, that you don't appreciate that type of behavior or talk and that you may well be losing respect for them.

These are but a few thoughts on the concept of dignity. It begins with us and from there moves outward to others. When we combine both honor and dignity in our lives, we begin to see changes in the way people think about us and treat us. Who doesn't want to be treated better? Begin by treating yourself better, believing the best of yourself, eliminating the negative tapes and behavior that is so destructive, and living a life of goodness and truth and honor.

Anecdote time. When I was beginning my career in law enforcement, I was taken aside by an older, wiser officer who was "experienced" in life. He was somewhat cerebral, which suited me fine. In taking me aside, he said, among other things, that the key to a successful career and life outside the job was to treat people like I wanted to be treated, to treat them with patience, respect, and dignity. He said that demeaning and controlling behavior had no place in enforcement. He said that there were going to be times when I would have to take control of a given situation, but that I should do so with wisdom, confidence, and poise, being in control of myself before I was to take control of the situation. Above all else, he said, treat the "clientele" with dignity first, patiently, yet firmly, giving them every opportunity to comply before taking action. That advice served me well throughout my career and life. When things have fallen apart, I have noticed that my thoughts and behavior have usually fallen apart first.

Another personal anecdote. When I was in high school, our football team was decimated by injuries and many were "going both ways," that is, playing both on offense and defense. One of our healthy defensive backs was a shorter individual who had reasonable skills but who opposing quarterbacks seemed to exploit. The coach came to another player, taller, who was also fairly athletic but who only played on offense. I overheard a conversation between him and the coach prior to one game.

The coach said, "I'm going to start you on defense tomorrow."

Tall guy: "What about (short guy, who will remain nameless)?"

Coach: "I want you to be ready."

Tall Guy: "I would love to start, but (short guy) has started all season, and it wouldn't be fair to him to pull him from starting. I would rather he started."

Coach: "Hmm. If that's what you think and want, then fine, just be ready to go."

I couldn't believe what I was hearing. First, no one contradicted the coach; he was a very strong personality who usually got what he wanted. Second, I thought, *Who wouldn't want to start both ways, to never come off the field? Is he afraid?* This stuck with me all night. Then just before dozing off, it hit me: Fear had nothing to do with it. He had his team in mind, specifically his teammate. It was so much more about others, or his team and teammate, than it was about him. Who knows? It could have been devastating to the short guy, wrecking his confidence and self-worth. It was more important for tall guy to see his teammate emotionally strong than potentially weakened. The interesting thing is the two of them were not even close by any stretch of the imagination. I don't recall hearing them say anything more than "Hi" to each other. That story has, oddly enough, stuck with me all these years, wondering what happened to those two guys. We may never know. What I do know is that, although I wasn't particularly fond of the tall guy, his behavior in that situation has stuck with me all these years. Such a small thing in the big scheme of things, yet such an honorable, selfless thing to do. Such is the nature of honor. Done in quiet selflessness, with others in mind. No fanfare. Rooted in humility. Honor. Then some putz comes along writing a book who happened to overhear everything and blabs it to the world. Nice.

Then there is the Bible story of Job. As the story goes, God allowed Satan to have his way with Job and his family a couple of times. It got messy. So messy, in fact, that Job's wife said to him, "Curse God and die." Even after losing everything—family, possessions, and health—Job responded with, "Shall we indeed accept good from God and not accept adversity?" By all accounts, Job was an honorable man who lived with integrity. Such is the nature of honor.

Treating ourselves and others with honor and dignity not only opens our spirit but allows us to see the endless possibilities available in life. It becomes easy to feel good about ourselves when we start doing things right, at the right time, and doing the right things. This includes the way we view others, as well as treating others with honor and dignity. But it begins with us. And it begins in the heart. For some people, it seems to come naturally. With others, it is a foreign concept, one they need to mindfully and intentionally work on.

Points to Ponder

1. *Are there areas in your inner life where, for expediency sake, you take shortcuts or make compromises?*

2. *Do you value yourself and others enough to treat yourself and them with dignity and respect?*

3. *In what situations in life do you find the most difficulty acting honorably?*

Chapter 30
FAITHFUL AND LOYAL

These two topics lead me to reminisce about my old dog. She was a purebred black lab. Faithful and loyal to the core. She would do anything I asked of her. She jumped fences six feet high, climbed trees, and would let nothing come between me and her pleasing me. And she loved her ball. It was her "leash." I could take her anywhere off leash as long as I had her ball in my hand. She would be so fixated on it that she would run into stationary objects because she was constantly looking back at the ball in my hand.

One quick story about her. I told a guy at work about her, and he was the main dog handler for Customs. He came by to check her out, mainly to shut me up, as I was constantly lauding her behavior. Problem was she was getting a little too old to train; at five she was perhaps a little past her prime. When he came by, I put her in the garage and locked it. From there, I took her ball and rolled it from the house to the gate in the fence, where it rolled down the slope on the other side of the fence. I walked the long way around so as not to have her follow my scent. I then picked up the ball and launched it on the ground along the fence line on top of the slope. As the ball lost momentum, it rolled down the slope to the bottom. I walked around, picked up the ball and did the same thing. It rolled along the fence line until it ran out of momentum and rolled down into a blackberry bush, where it ended up out of sight. Then I walked the long way around to the garage and opened the door. I let her out, asked where her ball was and she got excited, checking out my hands but seeing them empty. She then ran, sniffing the ground, to the other side of the yard but found nothing of interest. She then crossed back to the side we were on, caught a scent right away, and bolted to the gate, nose to the ground. She ran out the gate and down the slope, sniffing all the way. Soon, she ran out of scent, hit the brakes, reversed, and picked up the scent at the fence line, running quickly, head bobbing from side to side with her nose seemingly in one massive inhale. Then something interesting happened: She once again ran out of scent, picked it up going down the slope, slowed at the bottom, and reversed back up the slope, always sniffing and always totally focused on finding the elusive ball. She followed the scent down the fence line to where the ball rolled down and into the blackberry bush, where she triumphantly picked up the ball and bolted back to us, where my buddy was picking up his jaw from the ground, blown away by that display.

The point of the story is multi-fold. First, the relationship between my dog and me was one of love and trust. This spawned a sense of loyalty between the dog and I that was very strong. I simply provided play for the dog and nurtured a sense of fun with her. I also fed her and provided shelter. I included her in much of my spare time, taking her with me when practical. She responded with a thumping tail that, oftentimes, caused a modicum of destruction and breakage, depending on what was close at "tail." Second, the love and trust manifested itself in the dog being "set off" with joy in seeing me or hearing my voice calling her. Although she wasn't as exuberant when we were doing obedience training, she faithfully went through the motions, perhaps understanding that the sooner she completed these, the sooner her pay-off of playing with the ball happened. Then there was the whole area of obedience. This seemed to manifest itself in her being faithful to heeding my voice above all others. For example, if there were competing voices for her attention, she would always heed my voice and mine only. That's not to say she wouldn't go to others and listen to them, but not if I was around. She would faithfully listen and discern who was talking, and if it was me, would obey faithfully and loyally. Man, I miss that dog.

Such are the relationships we find ourselves in. I am speaking of emotionally and spiritually healthy relationships. What does being faithful mean? It means, among other things, that we are reliable, consistent. It means that we will get the job done, regardless of the circumstances and adversity we may face. We may not like what we are doing; we simply do it because it needs to be done. Being faithful has, at its root, love, which also means there is humility involved. Focusing on love, we are faithful to those we love. We give of ourselves to others or to a cause because we love them or love the cause we are affiliated with. We will do whatever it takes to get the job done. Fidelity also comes to mind in discussing being faithful, and this will lead to our discussion on being loyal. It should also be mentioned that faithful also means being full of faith, but that is a discussion for a later date.

Being faithful implies commitment. I am committed to do what it takes to maintain my love relationship with my wife. If we weren't committed to one another, we wouldn't be together after thirty-eight years of marriage. Remember, I went off the proverbial deep end in addiction for nearly seven years, yet it was nearly ten years after she left me that we are together again and have a healthier relationship now than we ever had. Allow me to dispel the "Why should I change?" myth, or the "I'm not changing for anyone; they can accept the way I am" myth once and for all. If our words, behaviors, heart, and spirit aren't going to change, what is the point of even being here? For one thing, time and experience change the way we think and act. If we want to get along with society in general, change is mandatory; no one is perfect. This is not to be mistaken with "people pleasing." It is what used to be referred to as common sense. We adapt our behavior in order not to be at odds with everyone.

In my case, I am fairly certain (read: absolutely positive) that my wife would not have taken me back if I was still stuck in addiction and displaying addictive behavior. Clearly, I am not that good of a catch that she absolutely had to be with me. It also speaks to her independence. She didn't *need* me, much to my chagrin and wounded ego. When I began to change my ways and grow up, leaving the homeless drug addiction behind, becoming a better man than she knew long before she left, she began to change. Today, we are two changed individuals living together, mostly happily ever after. Indeed, upon closer reflection, we are closer and more spiritually intimate than we have ever been, mainly because I am no longer an immature child in adult clothes, not to put too fine a point on it.

The point in this whole discourse is that, through all the crap that I went through, she remained faithful to me. No boyfriends or affairs. Of course, the same was true of me. She lived alone, praying for the day that I would come to my senses, leave the addiction, and return to normal. Faithful and loyal. It is important to provide a working definition of "loyal." The dictionary says it is the "giving or showing firm and constant support or allegiance to a person or institution." I am thinking here of sports, specifically the Vancouver Canuck hockey fans, or Cleveland Browns football fans (my tongue firmly planted in my cheek). The point being, no matter how bad the team does, the loyal fans show up every game, every season, hoping for the best. The term "diehard" comes to mind. You get my point. My wife was like that: She continued believing the best would happen until it finally did happen. Today, we celebrate this victory.

Points to Ponder

1. *Is "faithful" a word that others, or we, would use to describe ourselves? If not, how would we describe ourselves?*

2. *What are some little things that we can be faithful in that we may not have been up to now?*

3. *What, or to whom, do we show our love and devotion?*

Chapter 31
THANKFULNESS

I will develop and maintain a spirit of gratitude,
giving thanks for everything I receive and
every circumstance that I encounter

This is one of the most underrated spiritual traits. It is often overlooked in life. Why is this so? What does it mean to be thankful? To have gratitude? When should we be thankful and for what should we be grateful?

We have come a long way, culturally, from when our forebears set up a day, specifically, to give thanks for the blessings that they felt they received from their creator. Today, on that day we set aside for Thanksgiving, we have parades, football games are played, the flames of rivalries are stoked for another year, some will experience the joy of victory and others the agony of defeat. Then comes the meal. Despite successes or failures on the field, or in the stands, there is a time for celebration around the table. Family is gathered, food spread, and we dig in. The family will then reminisce, fondly looking back at those times of yore when things seemed to be fairly perfect. With any luck at all, there will be no fights, no fisticuffs, no one will storm out of the house, and everyone will have a great time. This seems to have become the ideal in North America. At least, this is what the movies would have us believe.

The reality is that not all families get together for the holidays. If they do, tensions may run very high due to some past hurt or painful experience growing up. Arguments and fights ensue. The last thing on anyone's mind is thankfulness. In the United States, the day after Thanksgiving is a huge shopping day known as *Black Friday.* Mobs invade popular shops, stores, and malls, everyone seeking the perfect gift at the best price. Oddly enough, not all items purchased are for others. Not to stray too far off topic, but our day of thanksgiving is past, and we are moving on to more important things in life. Thus, for many, Thanksgiving Day is a painful reminder of a troubled past, hurt feelings, damaged emotions, and … indigestion.

How has our North American culture changed? And how can we change it back? It would seem that we have become a very entitled lot here in the New World. In my humble opinion, *entitlement* seems to be the antithesis, or opposite, of thankfulness. With this entitlement comes an inner sense of having to be right, leaving no room for dissension or disagreement. Indeed, we would *rather be right than happy.* Everything then becomes a battle to convert everyone to our way of thinking or destroy them in the process.

One of the more significant differences in our society today is that many have not had to suffer great hardship, or a prolonged hardship, leading to changes in the way we view the world around us. Very few of us have experienced ongoing persecution for our beliefs. As a result, we have gone beyond taking things for granted and have adopted a sense of entitlement. We are owed an enriched lifestyle. We are owed a college education, a good job, a nice house and car. And then there are those who don't feel like they are entitled to a good job; they simply want the good income without having to work for it.

Personally, I have adopted a spirit of thanksgiving and gratitude *every day.* Like the old song says, *Every day above ground is a good day.* I am thankful that I have fresh air to breathe, *that I am physically capable to breathe,* that I have fresh water to drink, that I have food to eat when I want to eat—with none going to waste, by the way—that I have a place to live and a car to drive, and that I have clothes to wear (not always the most stylish, but they fit). My point is simple: My needs are met, and I am thankful for that.

Points to Ponder

1. *List three things that you are thankful for.*

2. *List three things that you believe you are entitled to have.*

Get Real

Perhaps a better, more appropriate, heading would be "be real." Of course, the "be real" title is simply my boycotting pop-culture psycho-babble. The pop-culture title would read, "be the authentic you." This is my final encouragement and exhortation to you. Let people see the real you, not the fake, public persona with walls up, masks on, never coming out, never letting anyone in. Pack that fake person away in the cellar, and don't let them out. Cultivate and develop the inner person, your soul and spirit.

The world doesn't have any trouble cultivating and developing its share of fake people. It would seem gravity affects the spirit as well as the physical person. What I mean is simply that negative behavior has a tendency of begetting more negative behavior. We can see the effects of this with the advent of masked protestors violently disrupting peaceful demonstrations. It would seem as though there are those on both sides of whatever is being protested who show up only to fight with their counterparts. Of course, it is the bad apples from each camp that cause the trouble. We have even seen the rise of the "masked" protestor, and by masked I am referring to physical face coverings and not the metaphorical masks we discussed earlier.

What has caused this demise in societal decency? What gives people the perceived right to physically impose their beliefs on others? What has happened to us that we now spew vitriol and hate to further our point of view? It would seem as though the face covering, or mask, is a substitute for the keyboard and monitor that people hide behind when they promote their fake persona. And therein lies the problem. As long as we can hide, to *not* be seen, we will be safe. Unfortunately, following the gravitational pull of bad behavior, we will one day see the inhibitions go by the wayside and true fascism will rear its ugly head.

If ever there was a time to be congruent in our lives, it is now. Our behavior should be no different in public than in private. Our words should be the same whether we are at work, at play, or at home. There should be no need to hide behind masks, real or otherwise, in order to fulfill our purpose in life.

This naturally leads to the next question: "What kind of purpose in life requires the wearing of a mask to hide our identity to advance our cause?" Generally, only *fake* purposes require subterfuge and deceit. But if we were to get real, we will see that it is not really about purposes and causes. It is about a sense of insecurity and the fear of being known. People aren't happy with themselves, with their perceived lot in life, so they seek acceptance in unhealthy ways and with other unhealthy people. People need to face their inner demons, exorcise them, and become the real people they were created to be.

Conclusion

One of the mottos in my life is this: "Build a bridge and get over it." So often our pre-conceived notions on spirituality are just that: our pre-conceived notions. It is my contention that spirituality is something we are all born with. It can be nurtured or ignored as life goes on. Ignoring it is the default; nurturing is the intentionality that is required to cultivate it. If you find God, who is Spirit, along the way, great. If you choose to ignore God but cultivate your spirit nonetheless, that's good too. There are worse things than following the precepts set out in this book.

If I can close with one final thought, it is this: Don't live as a victim; live as a victor. Leave the blame game, take responsibility for your words and actions, and begin to look within to achieve your goals and dreams. It's going to take some work. Change will be both inevitable and painful, but you are worth it. Of course, I would be remiss if I didn't mention humility in closing. Don't look out only for your own interests but in humility consider others better than yourself. What I am saying is two-fold: First, have your own interests. That is okay. Second, live in true humility with the world around you. Your spirit can be healed, restored, and thrive in the new you. You will be better off for it, and the world will be better with the "new" you in it.

About the Author

Tyler Walton is a Canadian husband, father of two, and grandfather of four. Growing up, he was heavily involved in sports, and attended and graduated from seminary at Trinity Western University in Langley, British Columbia. He is a retired Immigration Officer/Canadian Border Services Officer, currently living in Langley. He has overcome addiction and homelessness, reclaimed the gift of his inner spirit, and now writes and speaks about it, inspiring audiences of all ages.

Visit Tyler at tylergwalton.com or send an email on how to book him to speak at your school, group, business, or conference. mailto:tyler@tylergwalton.com

Can You Help?

Thank You for Reading My Book!

I really appreciate all of your feedback,
and I love hearing what you have to say.

I need your input to make the next version
of this book and my future books better.

Please leave me an honest review on Amazon,
letting me know what you thought of the book.

Thanks so much!

Tyler G. Walton

CPSIA information can be obtained
at www.ICGtesting.com
Printed in the USA
BVHW040352080122
625105BV00006B/99